Becoming Emotionally Intelligent

Catherine Corrie

In the face of your unswerving commitment to grow,
students will emerge like butterflies from a chrysalis;
they will become the leaders of their own lives.

Joshua Freedman

Published by
Network Educational Press Ltd
PO Box 635
Stafford
ST16 1BF
www.networkpress.co.uk

Managing Editor: Janice Baiton
Design: Neil Hawkins – Network Educational Press Ltd
Illustrations: Anita Geaney
Cover illustration: Kerry Ingham
Printed in Great Britain by MPG Books Ltd, Bodmin, Cornwall

Contents

Foreword

I turned to Catherine and, off the cuff, said, 'I wish I were more emotionally connected to this group.' Instead of a light response, she stopped and thought.

'What would you have to give up in order to do that?' She asked with more than words – I could feel that she was genuinely listening, that she was 100 per cent concerned and that my answer was important.

I was not expecting a 'real' answer, I certainly was not expecting wisdom. For me it was a passing comment in a long week of training together. We were co-facilitating an emotional intelligence course – content that I had been delivering around the globe, and I had reached the point where in some ways I was not fully engaging my own emotions in my work as a teacher.

In that moment, I saw why Catherine has been a transformative trainer for so many teachers. It is not so much her endless 'bag of tricks' – the strategies every teacher develops over the years – rather it is her own emotional depth, her ability to see beyond the surface and listen for something more in each of us.

In this book you will encounter some of that feeling. Liberally seasoned with case studies and exercises, this book will enable you to appreciate this experience. As you read, imagine your own classroom, your school – all schools – as a place where students can fully come to life, a place which invites them to develop their best selves.

As Catherine says, 'Emotional Intelligence is not something you do in your head, it is not a mind experience, it is an emotional, physical, mental and spiritual experience.' So this is not just a book of ideas – in fact, if you only read it, you will miss the point. This is a book to experience. Do the exercises, don't just read them. Call a friend and share the results. Talk to your students and have them try out the questions. Go deeper.

The result will be more clarity about your own thoughts, feelings and actions – an increased awareness of your patterns and ability to make meaningful choices. If you bring this awareness to your classroom, it will change your students. Catherine likes to ask, 'Who are you being as you do this work?' It turns out that the answer matters deeply and that you can choose who you are as a teacher. You can choose to be the teacher who awakens the hidden greatness in every student, or inspires the next generation of teachers. It starts with you choosing to keep learning.

As Catherine writes,

> Children of all ages are very perceptive. They observe, both consciously and unconsciously, and they model the behaviours they see. If you are to support the children in your school to become emotionally intelligent, your honesty with your emotions, your care with others' emotions, the words you choose to use and how you follow-through on commitments are all integral to the children's learning.

Children do not expect us to be perfect and never make mistakes, but they have little tolerance of hypocrisy, so whatever we are asking of them, we must be prepared to ask more of ourselves.

Teachers are overwhelmed, undersupported and overextended – I have not met one teacher in the world who welcomes 'adding something new' to the workload. So the idea of asking more of yourself may seem like a ridiculous proposition. Yet if you do it, the results will astound you. Not only will you work harder, but you will also relish it. It means your job will become harder. Your students will start asking real questions, which means you will have to think more deeply to answer. They will do remarkable work, which means you will have to stretch intellectually to keep them learning. They will love school, which means you will have to be more present to feed that hunger. And your teaching will bring you more delight, more energy, more sorrow, more joy, more fear, more power and more wonder than ever before.

In that week of training together, Catherine shared her experiences with me and my family, we talked a lot about this book – about the challenge for someone who does not see herself as a writer, about the need for more materials that inspire teachers and about the urgency of this work. My wife, who is also a teacher, and I both saw so much in Catherine's experiences – a richness that would enable any teacher to add depth and heart to a classroom. So it is with great pleasure that I see *Becoming Emotionally Intelligent* appearing in print and, as you read on, I invite you to discover new resources for Emotional Wisdom.

Joshua Freedman
Director of Programs, Six Seconds Emotional Intelligence Network

Acknowledgements

This is my first book and I have a number of people I wish to acknowledge.

Glen Corrie for his love, support and encouragement, particularly during the four years of my teacher training.

Dr Pat Wade who made it clear to me during my training as a teacher that schools could be places where the whole child could be supported to grow.

Philip Mordy, my first headteacher and a great friend, for being a great role model, putting up with my wild ideas, allowing me to grow and develop my teaching in a way that was true to my beliefs and values and for always putting the children first.

Bruno Grzegorzak who taught me the importance of consistency and humour in my first year of teaching.

Derek Hayward for the value he places in developing a supportive learning environment for the children, staff and parents in his school and for allowing me to be part of that on-going vision.

Mary Cassidy for being the person who started me off in my work with teachers and believed in me.

Nicky Anastasiou for her continual support and encouragement of the work I do and for getting as excited as I do when adults remember what it is like to be a child.

Mary Aver, my mentor and spiritual teacher, for the way she has helped me to develop my own emotional and spiritual intelligence.

Paola Prina for helping me to break my own limiting behaviour patterns and be more true to myself.

Sally Davies, Bob Fletcher and Roz Hancell for their generosity in reading the very early draft of the book and giving me very useful feedback.

Jim Houghton for asking me to write this book and allowing me to fully express the things I feel passionately about.

Janice Baiton for all the work she has put into editing this book and for the thoughtful way she supported me throughout this whole process.

Anita Geaney for the beautiful way she has illustrated the thoughts and ideas in this book and for being such a fantastic sister.

Luke, Matthew and Olivia, my children, for being my greatest teachers and for the way they have encouraged me in everything I have done.

Alice my beautiful and amazing granddaughter for being my inspiration.

My mother and father and all the friends and family who have kept me going during the writing of this book, thank you for the phone calls and the emails that always came just at the right moment.

Josh Freedman, for your friendship and his support with this book and for answering all my 'help!' emails.

All the children mentioned in this book and all the other children I have taught and worked with, thank you for your love, for all the laughs and for all you have taught me.

Chapter 1

Introduction: Emotional Intelligence

What to expect from this book

Andrew has come into Year 6. He has a reputation for being angry, violent and abusive, plus he has personal hygiene problems and smells very strongly of stale urine. He either refuses to do his work and becomes abusive, or he rips his work up and throws it in the bin. In Year 5 he spent most of his time being sent to various classrooms because his teacher could not cope with him in the room. The other children in the class will not go near him, or sit on the same table as him, or even touch things he has touched.

This is a real example of one child I had in my class and I know that there are many 'teachers' who have been in a similar position.

When I mention 'teachers' in this book I mean it in the broadest sense; if we are around children in our work or in our homes we are unconsciously or consciously teaching them all the time, so we are all teachers.

If I had not spent years working on my own Emotional Intelligence, I, too, would have had great difficulty keeping Andrew in the room and teaching him, and he may well have ended up excluded before the end of Year 6. Even with the skills and understanding I had developed, it was not always easy. However, by Christmas he had begun to trust me and the rest of the class. Every child in the class sent him a Christmas card and when he told me, he was crying because nothing like that had ever happened to him before. He said, 'I would love to send them one back but I don't have any money.' So I went out and bought him a box of cheap cards.

By Easter, Andrew was able to manage his anger and had stopped harming people, including himself. The children in the class supported him instead of 'winding him up' and making it impossible for him to develop self-control. He had disclosed to me the truth about his home life and was now on the 'at risk register' with social services. By the end of the year he had done really well in his tests, had several good friends, was my greatest helper, smiled a lot of the time and was optimistic about secondary school. Most of all he *knew* that I cared about him a great deal and that I always would.

Imagine what this experience has done for Andrew and the rest of his classmates. They have witnessed and been part of a transformation; they have learned to be tolerant, accepting, thoughtful, supportive, self-controlled, kind and generous.

So how did I do it?

Well, by the time you get to the end of this book, you will know how. Not only will you *know*, but you will also *understand* and have the *tools* and the *confidence* to model the sort of behaviour that Andrew and many children like him have never consistently experienced from anyone.

You can *change* a child's life just by being *who you are,* and so I ask you to consider what sort of *change* you would choose to create. And are *you being that person* consistently right now?

The biggest gift I could *ever* give Andrew is the gift I want to give everyone I meet – to see the beauty of the person, even when their behaviour is not outwardly showing that beauty.

At a recent wedding I heard this stated so well in one of the readings, it said, 'May you both remember the beauty of the other, even when they themselves forget it, and see the beauty of who you are reflected in each other's eyes.'

This is not an easy task when the person is behaving in a way that is damaging or hurting you or others. However, this is at the heart of Emotional Intelligence.

It is easy to remember the love or care we have for people when they are behaving as we would wish them to. Whether it is our own children/partners, or the children/adults who work with us, it is the same – when things are going the way we want, it is easy to behave as we would wish. The time we need to be Emotionally Intelligent is when things are not going as we would wish, when people are behaving in a way that is difficult, when life is sending things our way that are hard to manage.

To go back to Andrew, listed below are the Knowledge, Understanding, Skills and Attitudes I needed to achieve my end result.

- ❀ Basing my attitude on my belief that all children are beautiful and that their behaviour is only a response or a reaction to their environment.
- ❀ Knowing my own behaviour patterns well enough to understand what might cause me to respond in a way which would be disrespectful or damaging.
- ❀ Developing skills to help me be in control of my behaviour and responses even when dealing with Andrew was really difficult.
- ❀ Knowing how to maintain my boundaries in a way that respected both of us.
- ❀ Understanding Andrew's emotional state and thus his responses.

❀ Being skilful at staying within my own power, not giving it to Andrew and not taking his.

❀ Helping him to understand the result of his behaviour without causing him to feel like a bad person – just a good person who is getting it wrong at the moment.

❀ Being able to communicate my feelings, my values and my vision to Andrew in a way he would understand.

The above Knowledge, Understanding, Skills and Attitudes are what this book is about.

What is Emotional Intelligence?

Emotional Intelligence is a way of understanding and shaping how we think, feel and act. Our personality or ego is made up of our emotional, physical and mental bodies and everyone has a unique combination of these. Although we all feel *similar* emotions (such as anger, joy, upset, pain, excitement and passion), have *similar* bodies (with a head, limbs, heart, lungs and blood), and have minds with *similar* thoughts, each of these is put together *differently*, which is what makes everyone an individual.

In addition, some people believe humans have what can be referred to as a soul. Again each one is unique and yet is a part of the whole. Understanding our soul and how it connects and interacts with the personality could be called Spiritual Intelligence (see Chapter 12). Our emotions are affected *by* our thoughts and *by* our physical bodies, and, at the same time, those emotions *affect* our thoughts and our physical bodies. There is no separation between these three parts of us.

Our Intellectual Intelligence allows us to solve logical problems. According to Zohar and Marshall our Spiritual Intelligence allows us to 'address and solve problems of meaning and value … to place our lives in a wider, richer, meaning-giving context.'[1] Our Emotional Intelligence is the bridge between the two. It is difficult to place our lives in a wider, richer context if we are constantly run by our emotions. My Intellectual Intelligence may tell me I am overweight and that this is not healthy, and although I value my health in a very spiritual way, I still may be ruled by the emotional responses that cause me to overeat.

Why Emotional Intelligence is important in the classroom

 Don't worry that your children don't listen to you. Worry that they are watching everything you do.

Weatherley

Children learn from the way the significant adults around them are being and not so much from what they are saying. When we as teachers or carers are living or working with children, the person we are being and the behaviours we demonstrate *every day* play as large a part in the educative process as the content of what we are teaching.

Children of all ages are very perceptive. They observe, both consciously and unconsciously, and they model the behaviours they see. If, as teachers, you are to support the children in your school to become emotionally intelligent, your honesty with your emotions, your care with others' emotions, the words you choose to use and how you follow through on commitments are all integral to children's learning. Children do not expect teachers to be perfect and never make mistakes, but they have little tolerance of hypocrisy, so whatever we ask of them, we must be prepared to ask more of ourselves.

Even if all the correct learning resources are put into place and children are allowed to access the curriculum in a way that supports them, there will still be children who have, for a variety of reasons, behaviour patterns or negative beliefs about themselves that inhibit them from learning. Unless we understand their needs and can support them, they may well decide they are failures and just give up. Many children have done that simply because no one understood the nature of their internal environment and how it was affecting their learning behaviour.

Developing Emotional Intelligence improves self-awareness, motivation, empathy, recognition of choices and accountability. Developing skills in these leads to greater esteem, higher motivation, optimistic thinking, less violence, more responsibility, and strong and supportive communities, including classrooms and schools.

In the last decade or so, science has discovered a tremendous amount about the role emotions play in our lives.

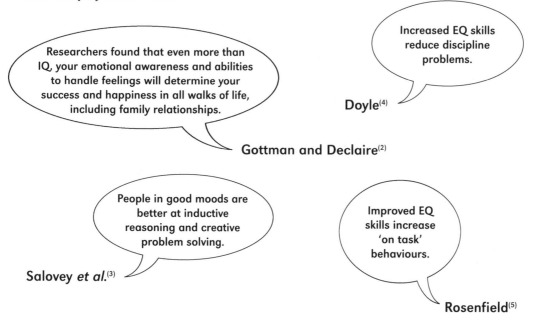

Researchers found that even more than IQ, your emotional awareness and abilities to handle feelings will determine your success and happiness in all walks of life, including family relationships.

Gottman and Declaire[2]

Increased EQ skills reduce discipline problems.

Doyle[4]

People in good moods are better at inductive reasoning and creative problem solving.

Salovey et al.[3]

Improved EQ skills increase 'on task' behaviours.

Rosenfield[5]

Research suggests Emotional Intelligence shapes as much as 70–80 per cent of success. It is essential for interpersonal and intrapersonal development and affects us in all our relationships – at home, school and socially.

Interpersonal Intelligence is the ability:

❀ to understand and work alongside others

❀ to empathise

❀ to be able to enter into another person's map of the world and see it from their perspective.

People skilled in this intelligence will be able to observe and respond to other people's behaviours and be able to motivate and inspire others.

Intrapersonal Intelligence is the ability:

❀ to reflect upon and understand oneself

❀ to recognise one's own feelings and the patterns of behaviour that have built up around them

❀ to understand cause and effect within oneself

❀ to know one's own values and be strongly aware when not acting in accord with them.

People skilled in this intelligence will be able to reflect on their own practices, ask themselves what part they have played in successes or failures, be responsible for themselves and not blame others for their shortcomings, know their strengths and their weaknesses and be willing to develop and set goals for themselves.

Understanding our own emotional systems and the connections between our thoughts, emotions and actions can affect and influence our day-to-day behaviours and our long-term development and growth.

A model of Emotional Intelligence

The three-part model below is a way of looking at Emotional Intelligence that can help us to understand and apply it.

1   Know ourselves
❀ Understand our emotions and our emotional responses.
❀ Understand the different roles we play.
❀ Understand the internal tapes that are our thoughts.
❀ Notice if our thoughts are optimistic or pessimistic.
❀ Notice the way we interpret and respond to our environment.
❀ Notice our behaviour patterns and how well they serve us.

    ❀ Know ourselves as learners and allow ourselves to learn and grow.

    ❀ Know the identity we have created and choose to keep it or develop it.

    ❀ Know we have the potential to be more than the identity we are now.

2 Make choices

    ❀ Choose how we feel and how we respond to our feelings.

    ❀ Choose our thoughts, so that they create the happiness we want.

    ❀ Choose to think optimistically.

    ❀ Choose interpretations that empower us.

    ❀ Choose to break and change the patterns that do not serve us.

    ❀ Choose to develop the areas that will help us to grow.

    ❀ Choose who we wish to be.

3 Make a positive difference to the world around us/develop Emotional Wisdom

    ❀ Move beyond the normal limits of our personalities to serve a greater goal.

    ❀ Act consistently in line with personal values and not emotional patterns.

    ❀ Act consistently out of love not fear.

    ❀ Be willing to be in service to others.

    ❀ Be able to consistently see the good in others.

    ❀ Be able to see the lessons we have learned from adversity.

    ❀ Be able to think optimistic thoughts which contribute to self and others.

    ❀ Have compassion and understanding for ourselves and others.

Emotional Wisdom

 Be the change you want to see in the world.
Mahatma Gandhi

Emotional Wisdom is the ability to use our Emotional Intelligence to contribute fully to our families, to our communities and to humanity as a whole. It enables us to choose 'who' we will be and to live our lives true to our higher values, not as a response to fear and survival.

It is so easy to say, 'It is awful that so many people are starving', 'It is dreadful that there are so many children who are unloved', 'It is dreadful what we are doing to the planet, but ...' and then put all sorts of reasons in the way of being responsible for changing things. We look at who we are and we say, 'I couldn't make any difference.'

Responses to such comments are: 'Who would you have to be to make a difference?' 'What do you really care about and feel passionate about?' 'Who would our children have to be to make a difference?' Using Emotional Intelligence and Emotional Wisdom, you could start creating that person now. Start becoming that person today and start supporting the children in your care to do the same.

We do not have to 'be' the culmination of our past experiences, the sum of our patterns of behaviour, which we have developed as an emotional response to fear, failure and disappointment. We can learn from our experiences and alter the patterns, select our responses and change our personality to become whom we choose to be, whom our Spiritual Intelligence would choose us to be.

How do I know if I am an emotionally intelligent teacher?

The creation of an emotionally intelligent classroom has to begin with the teachers. There are a variety of ways we can assess our Emotional Intelligence; some education authorities have come up with their own assessment tools, which can be useful in breaking down the components.

In the book *Self-Science: The Emotional Intelligent Curriculum*,[6] Freedman invites readers to consider how prepared they are for teaching the curriculum. The list below comes from his book. Ask yourself the questions and if, after consideration, there are areas you feel need development, read on. The following chapters will take you through exercises and reflections, and give information that will enable you to work successfully on any areas of the list.

Do I appreciate children?	Do I recognise and accept children's emotional and social needs? Am I child-centred rather than subject-centred?
Do I have self-knowledge?	Do I know enough about myself to help children learn about themselves?
Am I open?	Am I able to share my feelings and thoughts? Can I say, 'I don't know'?
Am I warm?	Do I show a friendly, caring manner? Am I relaxed in most situations? Do I help others feel relaxed? Do children feel I like them?
How accepting am I?	Do I accept others and myself? Do I see feelings – other people's and my own – as valid? Do I accept the positive and negative in all of us?
Do I show support?	Am I able to be an advocate for the child – even when I don't agree?
Am I flexible?	Can I alter a course of action? Can I flow with the mood of the class? Can I respond constructively to the unexpected? Can I creatively re-frame situations and put them in a new light?
Am I empathic?	Do I recognise the feelings that others have? Can I identify feelings clearly?
Do I show respect?	Do I listen to all points of view? Do I work to overcome my bias? Do I manage my feelings so I do not blame or defend?
Am I accountable?	Do I believe in natural consequences? Do I let children learn from their mistakes or do I rescue them?
Do I set and move towards goals?	Do I see the big picture? Do I give myself to the larger community? Do I have hope for the future?

The basic unit of human memory is information in context plus feeling.
Elias[7]

There is no separation of mind and emotions; emotions, thinking, and learning are all linked.
Jenson[8]

Conclusion

I have taken my experience as a mother, grandmother, teacher, play-leader, youth-worker, daughter, friend and human being, as well as all my years involved with courses on personal development, spiritual development, emotional development and neurological development, and I have written it as a book. It is full of stories, exercises, information and practical ideas. I hope it will cause you to laugh and cry and, most of all, I hope it will support you to be a model for the children and adults around you.

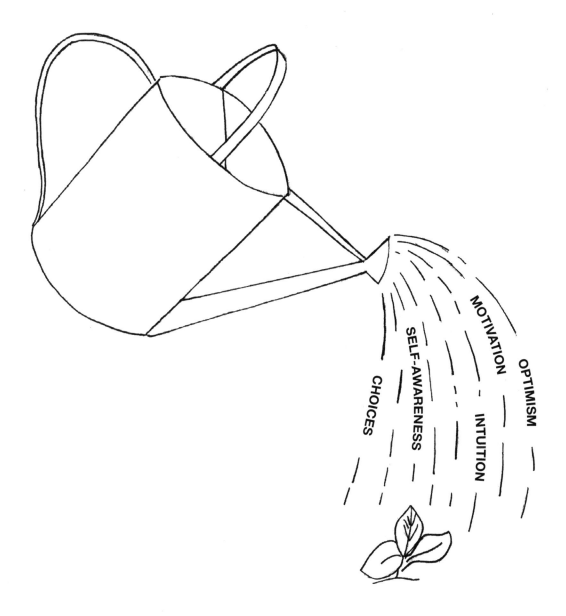

Chapter 2

Internal and external environment

A People Place

If this is not a place where tears are understood,
Where do I go to cry?
If this is not a place where my spirits can take wing,
Where do I go to fly?
If this is not a place where my questions can be asked,
Where do I go to seek?
If this is not a place where my feelings can be heard,
Where do I go to speak?
If this is not a place where you'll accept me as I am,
Where can I go to be?
If this is not a place where I can try to learn and grow,
Where can I be just me?

William J Crocker[1]

This poem epitomises the emotionally intelligent classroom. An emotionally intelligent classroom or school is, essentially, a people place. It is a place where tears and other emotions are understood and allowed, where enthusiasm is inspired, where all questions are welcomed as a source of learning, where all feelings, values and opinions are significant and where a child or adult can be accepted for who they are.

What are external and internal environments?

The external environment refers to everything outside a person. In the context of the classroom, the most important part of the environment is the other people: the teacher, other adult support and peers. The external environment also includes how people behave towards each other, how they speak and react, how they look at each other and what they think about each other. Other aspects are the size and layout of the physical space, the display, the sound, the resources available and how easily we can access and use them. All these elements affect learning on a moment-to-moment basis.

The internal environment refers to the thoughts, feelings, beliefs, values, patterns and memories we have within us. When pupils walk into a lesson, they walk in with particular feelings: they may be upset because someone has just said something nasty to them, they may be in a state of grief due to a loss or separation, they may be very excited and distracted because it is their birthday. They will also have a set of beliefs about the teacher, the subject, their own ability in this subject, other pupils' feelings towards them and so on. They will have a set of values about school, learning and its importance and the importance of the subject. In addition, they will have behaviour patterns that are triggered by memories and cause them to respond in a particular way, repeatedly, whenever that memory is activated.

This chapter explains the connection between the internal and external environments. It looks at how the internal environment is affected by the external environment and also how the internal environment affects the way we perceive the external environment. It could be argued that the external environment of the classroom is the same for all children. However, we know that children do not share the same experiences. What they think and feel about themselves, their teacher and their peers will influence how they interpret the external world.

> *Reality is what we take to be true.*
> *What we take to be true is what we believe.*
> *What we believe is based on our perceptions.*
> *What we perceive depends upon what we look for.*
> *What we look for depends upon what we think.*
> *What we think depends upon what we perceive.*
> *What we perceive determines what we believe.*
> *What we take to be true is our reality.*

Gary Zukav [2]

Connections between internal and external environment

Something happens

↓

You have a thought about it

↓

You feel something

↓

You react

↓

You see something, hear something

↓

You have a thought about it

↓

You react.

What happens here is that we attribute meaning to the external event. For example, your friend has said she will phone you on Friday evening, but she does not call.

You can choose the thought you have about this and give it whatever meaning you wish:

You think: 'She really doesn't care about me.'

The meaning will cause you to experience a particular emotion:

You feel: hurt and unimportant.

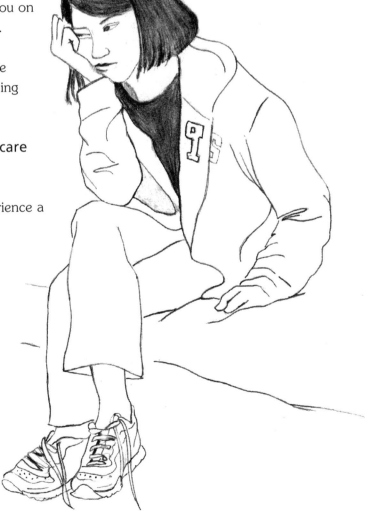

Alternatively, your friend does not phone on Friday as promised:

You think: 'I wonder why she hasn't phoned, I hope she's OK.'

You feel: concerned, or curious.

We could have a number of thoughts about any external experience, but it is the meaning we attribute to that experience which causes us to feel and then react.

So how important is the external environment? And why do we choose the thoughts we do? When we are deeply in love with someone the external environment begins to change; cold, dreary rooms can go unnoticed. When we are with people we feel really loved by or connected with, suddenly where we are is not so significant.

All teachers know how important it is to create a supportive learning environment. Yet it is clear that an environment which seems supportive for one child is not necessarily supportive for all. Teachers need to change the internal state of their learners so that the learners' internal environment is conducive to successful learning. The key to this is the link between our thoughts and the feelings created by those thoughts. Teachers need to help children think thoughts and make meanings and interpretations that aid their learning.

So how do teachers affect what pupils choose to make things mean? First, it is necessary to understand what causes us to think our thoughts.

The BASICS model and the internal and external environment

The BASICS model, as devised by Alistair Smith,[3] may be used to break down the different aspects of the internal and external environment in a way that is useful to educators. The model examines Belonging, Aspirations, Safety, Identity, Challenge and Success. How can the learner be helped to change their state so that they can learn even when life is difficult and their mother is sick, or their parents are fighting a lot? The first step is to make sense of the emotions taking place within the child and the causes and effects of those emotions.

Belonging

 Every now and then, take a good look at something not made with hands: a mountain, a star, the curve of a stream. There will come to you wisdom and patience, and above all, the assurance that you are not alone in the world.

Sidney Lovett

At the very early stages of our development, between the ages of 0 and 7, we have a strong desire to belong. We need to belong to the group/family in which we find ourselves. The small child is like an actor who has arrived on the stage, all the other players have their part and we need to find out ours so we can fit in and belong.

This stage is supposed to be over by the time we are 7; however, it usually lasts most of our lives. We seem to spend a lot of our time trying to belong.

The following exercise will inform you about the effects of this on our emotions and actions.

Exercise

1 Think back to the first time you felt that you did not belong, or felt outside, not connected. What is the earliest memory you have of this?

2 Remember yourself in the situation.
   a) What do you see?
   b) What do you hear?
   c) Can you remember what you thought and how you felt?
   d) What did this tell you about you as a person?

My first memory of not belonging happened in school. I was about six years old and feeling very excited about something. I rushed up to the teacher and started to tell him. He looked really annoyed and said, 'Not now, sit down.' This caused me to feel rejected and not really seen. It was as though I did not matter, that I was an irritation not a person. I remember looking around at the class and thinking, 'They all know, they know I don't matter.' The meaning I had attributed to that incident was 'I don't matter.' Of course the teacher had no idea he had caused that reaction.

They all know I don't matter...

Feeling that you do not matter has a very wide effect on your life, and once I had made that decision about myself, all the external environment did was prove it to me. When you believe you do not matter, you interpret external events in that light. Were I still to believe that, and my friend did not phone on Friday as promised, I would say, 'See I don't matter' and I would feel alone and unloved.

To sense belonging, we need to feel a connection between others and ourselves – to feel that we are really seen, that we are not just a pupil, not just an irritation.

Exercise

1 Think about your work colleagues and focus on the people with whom you feel a connection.

2 How does it feel to work alongside those people compared with those for whom you feel no connection?

3 What is it about those people that causes you to feel a connection with them?

4 What was it about them that made you connect with them in the first place?

5 Recollect your schooldays and focus on the teachers with whom you felt a connection. What effect did they have on your learning?

What you will notice in doing this exercise is how simple it is to connect. Sometimes it is just a hello or a smile. The people we connect with the most are those who do not judge us but will love us no matter what.

If we connect with every child we teach, they will feel a sense of belonging when they are around us. This will affect their ability to learn, their internal environments, how they interpret what we say and do, and their behaviour.

The children with whom we connect will not usually interpret our behaviour in a negative way. When we give them feedback about work or behaviour, they can hear it as useful. Whereas when we give feedback to a child or adult with whom we have no connection, they will almost certainly interpret it as negative.

So feeling connected affects what we make things mean and how we perceive the external environment.

Aspirations

 Our lives are shaped not as much by our experience, as by our expectations.
George Bernard Shaw

Case study: Joe's story

A pupil was having great difficulty with his temper. He reacted very quickly to what he interpreted as 'put-downs' and had been put on the special needs register for emotional and behavioural difficulties, reaching stage three. Several people from the behaviour unit had been called in to give support and the boy had been put on various target books and behaviour modification plans.

I came across him one day when he had been sent out of class for being rude to the support assistant. I sat and chatted with him for a while and we got around to talking about what he did in his spare time:

Becoming Emotionally Intelligent – Catherine Corrie

Joe: I play a lot of football.

Me: What do you want to be one day?

Joe : A goalie – I'm really good. I play for the local team every week.

Me: Have you ever been sent off for losing your temper?

Joe : (reluctantly) Yes, I was banned for a whole season once.

Me: Do you remember the last World Cup and what happened when one of the players lost his cool?

Joe : Yes, it lost us the cup.

Me: Well I think that from now on managers are going to be very careful who they sign up. There are lots of very talented players out there and they are going to want ones who can keep their cool and not get sent off for losing their temper. You see the opposition will quickly get to know your weak spots and your 'buttons' and they will make sure they keep pressing them until you lose it and get sent off.

Joe : So how do you learn to keep cool and not lose it? I don't know how to do it.

Joe was completely engaged in the conversation. I was tapping into his aspirations and using this to help him change his thoughts. Previously he had always been quick tempered, this was his learned reaction. Now he was open to the idea that maybe he could change, maybe there was something to learn and he could see how it would be helpful to him to learn it. There was something in it for him, something he valued.

Me: Well, when Miss X (the classroom assistant) does the things that press your buttons, you need to have a thought ready, something that will cause you to feel a different feeling, one that makes you feel powerful, or calm, or happy; any feeling that is not going to cause anger, frustration or fear.

So we looked at the thoughts he could have that would give him a different feeling. He liked the idea that the classroom assistant was now giving him a useful gift – as she constantly wound him up he could get a lot of practice at staying calm and managing his feelings. He decided that he would say to himself, 'She is the opposition and is trying to get me sent off.' (Not so different to being sent out of class.)

Since our first talk Joe has tried various thoughts. The ones that have worked the best have been thinking about all the teams he would like to be picked to play for, or simply thinking about football scores and league tables. Having different thoughts has changed his feelings and so his reactions have changed. In time his identity statement about himself, 'I'm quick tempered', will alter because he will have enough evidence to the contrary.

Tapping into Joe's aspirations allowed me to give him an area of thought that he found interesting and enticing enough to replace the thoughts that had previously resulted in the feelings of anger and revenge.

Instead of repeating the former patterns (every time the classroom assistant said something that sounded like a put-down, he would get angry), he now manages to change his thoughts and stay cool more often. He sees himself getting closer to his goal and not being sent off the pitch. Previously, when he had tried to suppress the anger (because he was on a target book and was not to be rude), he had felt humiliated and stupid. He thought it unfair that the classroom assistant got away with her put-downs and these thoughts only caused more anger.

Now that he regards her as practice for him, a chance to learn how to manage his emotional state, he feels pleased and powerful when he can let it go. He is seeing his environment differently, even though in reality it has not changed. Our aspirations can affect the meaning we give to the external environment and therefore affect our motivation and learning.

Safety

 Do you know what intelligence is? It is the capacity, surely, to think freely, without fear, without a formula, so that you begin to discover for yourself what is real, what is true; but if you are frightened, you will never be intelligent.

Krishnamurti

Our ability to feel safe within an external environment is very strongly affected by thoughts and feelings based on past experiences.

Catherine's story

My attempts at learning to swim provide a good analogy. I have had many teachers over the years who have tried to make it really safe for me. They have explained how I cannot sink with floats attached to me, or how they will hold me and not let me go. Some of these people I really trust and yet I have not felt safe enough to relax and just try: my body remains tense and I cannot float or swim. Yet I did manage to swim with two people – both were swimming instructors and I only met them once. Both told me so powerfully that I could do it, that I took my feet of the bottom and swam half way across the pool before my mind cut in saying 'You are going to drown' and panic started again. If I had been able to spend more time with either of these instructors, or if I had found another one who also believed in me and understood my fear, then I know I could have learned to swim.

Relate my story to a child in the classroom who does not feel safe enough to write. Many people whom he trusts may try to teach him, they may give him lots of 'floats' and tell him he cannot drown, but he still believes he will. You can give him word cards or books, computer programs, keep him safe by removing him from other children's laughter – all these and many more floats will not work until someone knows for sure that he can do it and fully understands his fear. Our fears do not need to be rational to be real to us. If a child has experienced strong feelings of failure – being different, being stupid, being shown up – he will not feel safe. The very thought of writing will fill his body with fear and the brain will send messages for the fight/flight hormone adrenaline to prepare the body: his heart-rate will increase, his muscles will go rigid, he may start to sweat and to run away.

Many children in class experience this fear at the mention of a spelling test, writing, PE, or whatever their personal fear may be. Giving them lots of 'floats' will not necessarily have any effect. Understanding that this fear is very real to them while also *knowing* that they can do it and, for a short time, getting them to believe it can make a difference. Neither of my two successful instructors told me not to be afraid, nor did they try to remove my fear; they just knew I could do it, they looked at me and I knew I could do it, and for a short while that knowledge kept me safe.

If your belief in someone is strong enough, it can affect their belief in themselves. If they only take their 'feet off the bottom' for a few moments, say 'YES! You did it!' and help them to do it again and again until they no longer need you. Do not remove the support of your belief in them until they fully believe in themselves. Also, very importantly, do not stop believing in them just because they take a long time to fully overcome their fear or because they fail some days and the fear is too great.

Even if the external environment is made as safe as possible in homes and in schools, people will still feel unsafe because of previous events and feelings. Experiencing the fear and carrying on anyway is what allows people to do great things. We all encounter fear at times and if we learn as children that fear is something that always stops us, then we may always be stopped in our lives.

Allowing children to develop courage is a gift for life; acknowledging their fear and believing in them, helping them to believe that they can do it, is what develops resilience.

Identity

 A person becomes an I through a you.

Martin Buber

The identity we build up over the early years of our life will shape the identity we keep. Events happen in the external environment and as small children we try to make sense of them. As we are very egocentric at this stage, we usually make them mean something about ourselves. We begin to build an identity based on how we fit into the world.

A small child is dressed up and ready to go to a party. She opens a can of fizzy drink and it sprays all over her and her beautiful dress. She looks at the nearest adult for a cue to tell her what to make it mean. The adult does not need to speak, the child will go by the feeling she gets from them. If an adult's body language, tone, breathing all give her the message that she has messed up, then she will make a meaning about herself to fit that; for example, 'I'm stupid.' If the adult's words do not match the message given with their body, the child will trust their body. That is what children do. Parents or anyone spending time with small babies will know that tiny, new-born babies pick up your feelings. They know when you are stressed, afraid, excited. You cannot hide your real feelings by saying things that are not true. Since babies are pre-verbal, there is less confusion – they just feel and respond.

As time goes by we build an identity based on all the meanings about ourselves that we have picked up from the external environment. Once the identity statements are in place, the external environment will be affected by the identity we have taken on. Decisions made as a small child on the basis of a look from their mother, father or teacher can affect how that child sees the world for the rest of their life. We all have thought patterns that match the identity we have taken on – we make meanings based on our identity.

THOUGHTS	FEELINGS
I don't belong	Lonely, rejected, abandoned
I'm not good enough	Sad, angry
I'm never going to amount to anything	Sad, angry, depressed, apathetic, self-hatred, anxious
I don't belong or I'm different	Afraid, paranoid, self-conscious, exposed
I'm stupid, I'm ugly	Helpless, worthless, self-hatred, angry
I'm not lovable	Unloved, worthless, angry

All the statements we make about ourselves have an effect on our interpretations, therefore they affect how we experience the external environment. If a child has an identity thought like 'I'm hopeless' and someone says 'What's that?' when looking at her painting, she might well interpret it as a put-down. Yet the same statement made to someone whose thought is 'I am talented and able', may be interpreted as an enquiry. Each child, in each classroom, experiences their environment in relation to the identity they have taken on.

Small children are like actors who have just arrived on a stage where all the other actors know their parts. They look around and watch the people they are with, and from the

reactions of others towards them, they build their identity/character. Thus a two-, three- or four-year-old child may well be influencing how you see the world today.

Challenge

 One shrinks or expands in proportion to one's courage.

Anaïs Nin

Challenge from an Emotional Intelligence perspective is related to a person's own response to a challenge. What I would find a challenge, another person might find boring, and someone else might find impossible.

Let us take as a model a simple EQ exercise that asks people to list the following:

Group 1 Comfort Zone	Group 2 Challenge Zone	Group 3 Stress Zone
Three things about themselves they would feel comfortable discussing openly in a group.	Three things about themselves they would not feel comfortable discussing but would be willing to do so.	Three things about themselves they would not be willing to discuss.

Group 2 asks a person to stretch his own comfort zone. When running this exercise, the leader needs to understand that the areas of discussion in the person's second group are a challenge. The leader needs to support the participant to make the environment as safe as possible. By choosing to work in this area, the participant will discover a great deal about himself: he will have to overcome fears and alter beliefs. If he was only to discuss the things in group one, the comfortable group, he will learn very little about himself.

However, if the leader tries to push the participant to discuss something in the third group, she will cause the fear level to rise and the person will go into a flight, fight, flock or freeze pattern. For those things to be discussed the person himself has to move them into group 2. Something has to cause him to say, 'This is not comfortable but I am willing.'

This exercise can be used as a model for working with learning of any kind. There are things a person would be willing to do and would feel comfortable doing them. Take a gymnast, for example; there will be moves that the gymnast is comfortable with but if he just goes on performing those, life will be safe but there will be very little challenge and, usually, he will get bored. Also very little growth and learning will be taking place. Normally the gymnast will be in the process of learning some new moves. These are moves that do not yet feel comfortable but, in the right environment, he is willing to try them. The gymnast is also willing to fail, maybe even get hurt a little, but he must believe he can do it otherwise the failure and hurt would stop him. So the challenge is high, it is exciting but so is the belief in his own ability to succeed. There also needs to be a strong belief in the coach and the coach's ability to teach. Asking the gymnast to perform a move that the gymnast felt was impossible for him, would be the same as discussing the things in group 3, which contains 'things I will not or cannot discuss'.

To enable the gymnast to try the move, the coach first has to find a way of shifting that move into group 2, 'challenging but I am willing to have a go'. A little fear is not usually a problem, but a lot can cause the fight, flight, flock or freeze patterns. There are a variety of ways teachers or coaches can ensure that learning is in group 2. One method may be changing the environment, for example, more mattresses to land on, breaking down the moves into smaller more manageable steps, or the coach performing the move alongside the pupil. Each person will need to be supported in a different way. The important point to remember in an Emotional Intelligence model is that the belief needs to change so that the point to be learned is now in the 'challenging but I am willing to have a go' group, and not the fear/stress 'I am not willing to do it' group.

Our job as teachers is to recognise which group we are working with for each pupil. We need to know which group is appropriate at which time. Sometimes it is helpful to give a child things to do that fall within the comfortable zone. This may be necessary to build up a learner's feeling of safety, yet we often work in the group 2 challenge zone. Here our job is to encourage and celebrate the courage and successes of the learner so that these things can be moved up to group 1. Lastly our job is to support the learner constantly to move things from group 3 into group 2, from what seems impossible to what seems a challenge but is possible. As teachers we never try to force learners to do things in group 3; this is what causes the stress/fear that inhibits learning.

Success

 I am not bound to win
But I am bound to be true,
I am not bound to succeed
But I am bound to live up to
What light I have.

Abraham Lincoln

Success is very much a feeling, or an emotional response. A person can appear successful to the outside world, but if they do not feel successful, it does not really count.

So what is it that allows us to feel successful? Is it about the end result or the amount of effort we have put into something? Or is it about something else entirely?

In schools the following conversation can often be heard between teachers and children:

Teacher:	'I just want you to try.'
Child:	'But I can't do it.'
Teacher:	'Just try.'

If the child thought he was going to be successful, he would be glad to try. What does he think being successful is?

When babies are learning to smile, blow bubbles, copy sounds or pick up things, what is it that keeps them going? Most babies do not give up and say, 'This is too hard, this picking things up, I'll let someone else do it for me.' Or do they? What is it about being successful that is so important to us?

Matthew's story

Many years ago as a young boy, my son started to learn the guitar. He asked someone to teach him the chords and then he would sit in his bedroom and practise. I would hear him getting furious and sometimes throwing the guitar across the room. In the end he gave up.

Recently he has started learning to play again and is having a lot of success. I asked him how it was different this time round. His reply was that, first, as a boy, he had a fantasy of being able to play like Jimi Hendrix or Eric Clapton very quickly. Second, he felt there were all sorts of expectations from his father and me. We had bought him the guitar after he had begged us for ages and he felt there was an expectation that he should practise and so practising became a chore. Third, he was taught chords and told to practise them. Yet even when he did and he could play them, he did not feel successful because the chords did not go together to make a tune he could recognise or one that he would choose to play. There was no sense of success.

Now he is teaching himself to play. He picked some simple tunes that he would like to be able to play, ones in which the chords are not too difficult. He practises playing and before very long he can begin to hear the tune. When what he plays begins to sound like a tune he recognises, he feels successful and this inspires him to continue practising.

It is so simple. The blocks that get in the way of our feeling successful are:

- ❀ being told or feeling we should – I should practise, I should be as good as him, I should be able to do this;

- ❀ unrealistic expectations, our own or others – focusing on the top of the mountain often has us give up because it always seems so far away;

- ❀ not seeing the point or the value – like learning to read but never being allowed to read any books you would enjoy.

I found that supporting Irish Traveller children to write their own storybooks gave them an immense feeling of success. They took the books home and read them to the family – the parents treasured the books and the children were seen as writers within their family. This feeling of being a successful writer changed their self-image and identity and, as we have already seen, the identity statements you make about yourself will affect the way you interact with your environment.

 If one focuses only on the journey's end, completion always appears in the distance. This leads many to abandon their goals when obstacles arise or the path grows steep ... The Law of Process is nature's assurance that we can achieve nearly any goal, no matter how lofty, by breaking it down into small, sure steps.

Dan Millman

Exercise

1 Think about something you have learned to do, which you feel you do well and still enjoy doing.

2 Now think back to when you were learning to do it and ask yourself the following questions:
- ❀ Why did I learn it in the first place?
- ❀ What can I remember about how I was taught?
- ❀ What did I see, hear, feel, taste, touch?
- ❀ What did the other person/people do/say?
- ❀ When I was trying to learn what happened, when I made mistakes, how did others react? How did I react? How did I feel?
- ❀ Was I allowed to try it out lots of times? Was I rushed? Did I feel pressured?
- ❀ Were there any 'shoulds'?
- ❀ How did I feel successful?
- ❀ What did being able to do this say about me as a person?

If you write down your answers to this and the answers of about another 10 or more people and put the needs together, you have the internal and external environments necessary to enable successful learning.

If you are teaching someone and they are not being successful, the above exercise can be a very useful way of finding out some of the environmental issues (both internal and external) that affect their learning. While answering the above, they will give you information about: the things that cause them stress, the things that cause them safety, what motivates them, how they like to receive teaching, how much practice they like to have, if they want to be left alone and come to you or they want you to keep checking their progress. We can use what has already been successful, or as much of it as we can, to create more success in a different area. Learners begin to see that they are capable and they can be successful, they can change the way they see themselves and realise they need to create an internal and external environment that is conducive to success.

How do you create an environment that supports learner success?

Some more exercises and ideas are included here to help you begin using your Emotional Intelligence to create a supportive environment for your pupils. As teachers this requires us to look at our thoughts, values, opinions and beliefs. We need to be honest and open with ourselves and find out how much our lack of Emotional Intelligence has affected the learners around us.

Some of the questions are challenging and could create a fear reaction in you, and patterns of fight, flight or freeze may occur – you may just close the book and dismiss it, get angry and slam it, or just say, 'Oh, I don't know.' Hopefully none of these will happen and the following suggestions will begin the process of reflection and self-knowledge that is the first stage of Emotional Intelligence.

Step one: belonging and connection

Exercise

1 Write down the names of the children you work with. Notice the names you cannot remember and ask yourself, 'Do I feel a connection with those children?'

2 Go down the list of names, look at each one in turn and think about that child. What is the first thought you have about the child? What word comes to you that would describe how you see the child?

3 If that is the first thought you have about that child, what feeling does that raise in you and how do you respond when you feel that?

4 Now look at the list of thoughts and circle any thoughts you would hate people to be thinking about you. If you had to work every day with someone thinking that about you, how would it feel? Would you be likely to feel a connection with that person?

Becoming Emotionally Intelligent – Catherine Corrie

5 Would you feel comfortable receiving feedback from them? How would you interpret it? If you made a mistake, would you find it easy to ask them for help? If you were worried or upset, would you feel comfortable telling them?

6 Would a child feel connected with you if you were thinking that thought about them? Would they feel safe in your class – safe to share their feelings, to get it wrong sometimes, to give their opinions? Would it feel like a 'people place' to them?

Actions that support belonging and connection

❀ If you wish to change the environment for the children you teach, change the thoughts you have about them.

❀ Get to know the children you have written a negative or blocking thought about. See if you can find the child in there who wants to be accepted and wants someone to connect with them as they are now.

❀ Remember how it feels when you are with someone who wants to change you, someone who never quite accepts you as you are.

❀ Allow the memory of how that feels to be present in your body and think, 'Could I learn well when feeling like this?'

Step two: connecting to what they want and value

Exercise

1 Write down a list of the children you teach and beside their names write:

a) what you know about them

b) what they value

c) what they want to be

d) what they feel good at

e) what they love doing and why.

Actions that support children connecting to what they value

❀ Do you know the children you teach well enough to know what they value?

❀ How often do they get to choose?

❀ How are they being helped to learn the process of choosing well?

❀ Connect their reading, writing, maths, RE to their lives (which was always good primary education practice).

❀ Do not assume you know what is valuable to the children – find out.

Exercise

1 Plan some lessons in which the children can explore what they feel good at, what they love doing and what they value. (See examples of these in chapters 13–16.)

2 Plan some sessions on creating aspiration posters, so the children can show you and themselves what they want to be like.

Further actions that support children connecting to what they value

❀ Use what they aspire to (like Joe playing football for England) and connect it to the skills and understanding they are learning.

❀ Develop for yourself the notion of transferable skills and see where the skills the children are learning today will develop into the skills they want for the future.

❀ If you cannot connect what you are doing to what they value, then be flexible enough to look at what they value and change some of what you do.

Poster created by Ciara Geaney, age 8

Step three: believe in them

Exercise

1 Do the exercise in the section on success (see page 24) with any children you do not believe in.

2 Find out as much as possible about the things they are successful at and decide which ones you can adapt and use in your teaching.

Exercise

1 Think what made you successful when you were with some people and not others.

2 How does it feel to be encouraged by someone who really believes in you?

3 How does it feel to be encouraged by someone who does not really believe in you?

4 When does encouragement feel like pressure?

Actions that will affect your beliefs about children

❀ All you have to do is believe that, given the right circumstances, anyone can do almost anything.

❀ You just need to help them find out what they need, and you may not always be able to provide it. Can you still believe in the child and not blame them for being difficult?

❀ Can you believe in them even when they do not believe in themselves and have compassion and understanding for their difficulties?

❀ Can you accept them the way they are now and value the effort they make?

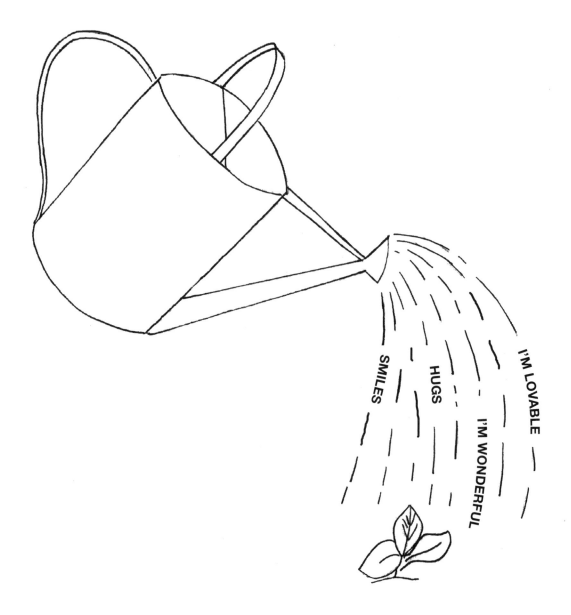

SMILES

HUGS

I'M WONDERFUL

I'M LOVABLE

Chapter 3

Understanding and managing behaviour

 Knowing others is intelligence;
Knowing yourself is true wisdom.
Mastering others is strength;
Mastering yourself is true power

Tao Te Ching

In order to understand or change behaviour patterns, it is important to know what beliefs and opinions are stored in our unconscious. The following exercises are designed to bring such thoughts into the conscious mind so you can assess them, consider any new information you read in this section and decide if you wish to change any of your beliefs.

Exercise

Ask yourself the following questions:

1 What is behaviour?

2 How do we learn our behaviours? Who do we learn them from?

3 How do we learn we have a choice about the way we behave?

Linking behaviour to Emotional Intelligence

First, there is instinctive behaviour. When a baby is born no one has to teach it to cry; crying is its way of communicating that it is hungry, wet, lonely, frightened or helpless. It is amazing how, even after a few days, new mothers begin to recognise the differences between the cries. Most mothers hear their baby's cry and know that he's hungry, or he wants a cuddle. Babies and mothers are not taught this behaviour and they have not modelled it; it is just instinctive. Children find a way to communicate their needs if there is someone really listening. When someone else is looking after them, they can get frustrated because the signals are not being picked up. This usually results in the crying getting louder and louder and the person feeling more and more concerned, because they cannot work out what the child needs.

Small babies only have needs; they are still not capable of having wants, which are beyond what they need for their survival.

The following exercise will enable you to think about what you do, as an adult, when you are in need, lonely, frightened, hungry, cold or need some human contact.

Exercise

Ask yourself the following questions:

1   How good are you at communicating your needs?

2   What do you do when the other person is not picking up the signal?

3   Do you still do your version of crying louder and louder, and does the other person do their version of frustration and concern because they do not know what you want?

It is often easier for a mother to listen to and distinguish the needs of her small baby than it is to distinguish the needs of her partner. Why is this so? Why do we seem to get worse, not better, at communicating our needs?

Do we teach our children, either at home or in school, how to communicate their needs effectively? Do they grow up to understand that it is the responsibility of the communicator to get their message understood? Do we teach them how to deal with not getting their needs met, or having to wait? Is emotional literacy (the ability to say how we feel in a way that is understood by the other person) or delayed gratification used or taught by most parents or teachers?

*As far as your self-control goes,
As far goes your freedom.*

Marie Ebner Von Eschenbach

Much difficult behaviour experienced in schools is the result of both adults and children trying to get what they want or what they need and not really knowing how to communicate successfully. The emotions experienced are often fear, anger, helplessness or variations of these. The response to those emotions is what causes the 'problem' behaviour. One reason for this is that we have usually developed a patterned response to most of these emotions and we no longer have conscious control over that response/behaviour.

Another reason is that one person's wants or needs sometimes clash with those of other people. When two people have very different wants or needs, there has to be very clear communication, a willingness to listen and a willingness to compromise. This is the basis of successful conflict resolution and indeed of successful relationships. We learn this type of behaviour though modelling – if adults consistently model clear communication, listening and compromise, then children will copy it.

The need to belong and be valued – its effects on behaviour

 We cannot escape fear. We can only transform it into a companion that accompanies us on all our exciting adventures.

Susan Jeffers

Exercise

Ask yourself the following questions:

1 Has anyone ever caused you to feel you were not OK?
2 Have you ever felt not approved of?
3 How did you react – did you keep trying to find ways to be accepted?
4 If it still didn't work, what did you do then?
5 How has this affected your life?

We can often cause children not to feel OK just by snapping at them, getting angry or impatient. Our early responses to this adult behaviour set up beliefs and values that lie at the heart of understanding our behaviour as an emotional response to the world we have created around us.

Chapter 2 examined how our thoughts and feelings affect the environment, and how they affect the way we perceive our environment.

Small babies are not aware of themselves as individuals with conscious will-power. As they become more and more attentive to their surroundings they realise that they are part of a group, family and any other significant groups. What becomes most important to them is a sense of belonging; they have to belong. It is vital and often babies who do not feel this sense of belonging and connection do not thrive.

They learn the power of sharing a belief with other people – they believe what the group seems to believe. They soon learn how painful it is to be excluded from the group and the group energy. They learn the code of behaviour and what is expected, and when they keep this code they have a sense of belonging, dignity and acceptance. When they do not feel a sense of connection or belonging, they feel insecure and alienated – they are not part of the group, not part of the tribe. As they do not have any sense of themselves as separate individuals yet, they feel lost and alone.

Children who do not feel connected will try to get noticed. They quickly realise that the best way to get noticed is to annoy people. They may 'show off', 'irritate', persistently 'annoy', or they may be very, very 'good.' They have to get noticed for something, get attention somehow, and that will be the only time they feel they exist and are part of the tribe. Anything is better than not being part of the tribe, because if you are not a part of it, then you do not exist, you disappear – you have to make your presence felt, you have to be noticed.

Another result of not feeling part of the tribe can be that a child comes to believe that nothing he does is good enough. If he has tried to fit in, tried to be part of the tribe/group, if he keeps trying to get it right and still people criticise him, then the child begins to feel inadequate. The resulting behaviour is usually negative power seeking. The child will often bully others and defy authority; his behaviour will often reflect a 'go on make me' or 'just you try and stop me' attitude.

If a child has done everything to get noticed and be good enough and yet still nothing he does makes any difference, he will begin to feel that he does not matter, that he does not count. Children who are given no boundaries often think they do not matter. I have found young children out in the streets alone late at night and asked, 'Won't someone be looking for you?' and been told, 'No, they don't care where I am.'

At the early stage of development, children's sense of power comes from belonging, being accepted and successfully connecting with those around them. Their sense of importance and value comes from knowing that they can contribute, that their presence matters and that they matter.

Sometimes they might get noticed, get attention and feel accepted for a while if they behave in certain ways, but inevitably being children they will probably do something to upset, disappoint or annoy the significant people around them. If this happens often, the child feels that just being themselves is not enough to earn love and acceptance. This could lead to them forming the following beliefs about themselves, I can't get it right, I'm not good enough, I'm not lovable.

The child will then try harder to get attention, gain acceptance and be liked, because they do not feel as if they are accepted just as they are, they need to do something so they will try to contribute. Unfortunately, washing the car with stones, making breakfast for every one at age 4, cleaning the bathroom with mum's toothbrush using toothpaste, polishing the family's shoes on the living room carpet, although done with the best intentions are contributions rarely valued by adults. However, in the early stage of development a child cannot understand this and feels they are not valued.

Some children try harder and harder to get it right and only manage to get it even more wrong.

Think of the emotional response that goes with these thoughts and beliefs. Hurt and anger – these very normal, very healthy emotions – often get twisted by the child into a need for revenge, to hurt back, to show the difference he can make. Children with such emotions often resent the sight of happy children, who seem to find it all so easy, and these children are often at the receiving end of the revenge behaviour.

All children really need is to feel important to someone, to feel they are accepted and valued for who they are.

Beliefs and how they affect our behaviour

 The real voyage of discovery consists not in seeking new landscapes but in having new eyes.

Marcel Proust

If as a child we believe we are not liked, then we can spend all our time proving it. If we feel we are not lovable, then we may make sure no one will ever love us. This is now our truth, this is how we see our place in the tribe. We are the unlovable ones, the outsiders, and we play this role to the very best of our ability. If this belief is developed when we are very young, then we would have no other sense of ourselves, we would only see ourselves in relation to our position in the tribe. But we would still feel – we would feel pain and anger – and we would still have needs. We would need to know we matter, need to feel valuable, significant and secure, need to feel loved.

As children often do not understand what they are feeling or why they are feeling it, they behave in very natural, very instinctive ways in response to their emotions and feelings: they get louder and louder, but no one seems to understand. Instead of helping them, instead of hearing their pain, their isolation, their need to be valued we, the adults, usually respond to the behaviour with rejection and anger. This causes children to feel more and more isolated – the more they react to the pain and anger of their isolation, the more they are pushed away.

Exercise

Ask yourself the following questions.

1 How many times have you felt isolated, or misunderstood? How have you responded?

2 Did the other person get the message or did they just get annoyed or confused?

3 Have you ever wished someone could be inside you for a moment so that they could understand?

Behaviour is not the problem but the child's solution to his problem

There is no such thing as negative emotions. There is nothing wrong with any of our emotions; they are just telling us something. What is often 'wrong' is our response to those emotions.

Exercise

When a child is showing you emotions like anger and pain because he feels insecure, alienated, insignificant, unloved, unaccepted, when the only way he knows how to show you what he needs is to respond to his emotions by getting attention, power over someone, revenge, angry, or proving no one likes him or cares about him ...

1 How do you respond?

2 Do you understand the communication? Or are you left feeling irritated, annoyed, helpless or frustrated because you do not know what they want or because it is getting in the way of what you want?

To teach children how to communicate their needs, we must be able to communicate ours. Even before this, we have to understand what it is we really need right now.

Exercise

Imagine you are a mother of two 13 or 14 year olds and you do a lot of the cooking, shopping and organising at home. You are the one whose job it is to remember that Jane has a dental appointment, or that Sheena has a dancing class. You also work and when you come home each evening your children have made toast, tea, sandwiches, etc., and have removed items of clothing and dropped them where ever they happen to be.

1 How do you feel?

2 What do you need?

3 How do you communicate those feelings and those needs?

Take a look at any situation in your life where you do not feel really heard, where the same thing keeps happening. This is caused by a lack of ability to communicate clearly what you want and what you feel.

Every day for 30 years a woman had been getting angry with her husband for leaving the toilet seat up. This behaviour has not helped her relationship with her husband, nor has it made any difference to her husband's habit of leaving the seat up, and yet she still kept doing the same thing. Why?

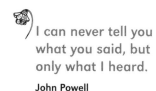

I can never tell you what you said, but only what I heard.

John Powell

Why do we keep repeating the same old patterns of behaviour? Why do we not learn to make our feelings and our needs heard successfully, particularly by those closest to us?

When my children were in their early teens, they used to behave in the way described earlier. My response at first was to come home and get really angry. I would stomp about banging cupboard doors and moaning out loud. Sometimes I would really blow and get furious, not because the house was any worse than normal, but because I was feeling tired and in need of some 'TLC'. At those times I would feel isolated, unappreciated and misunderstood. Didn't they see? Didn't they understand? How could they be so selfish?

Of course, they were not aware of my feelings and my needs. What they heard was mum moaning again and all they were doing was what most normal teenagers do – coming home from school, chilling out, relaxing, being at home.

How were they left feeling? Angry, frustrated, rejected, misunderstood.

We were all left feeling frustrated and misunderstood, and no one felt heard. The behaviour pattern I was acting out was one I had developed very early on. When as a child I felt those same feelings, I had a little tantrum, and I was still repeating that pattern.

> We cannot discover new oceans unless we have courage to lose sight of the shore.
>
> **André Gide**

I was more effective after I learned the power of the 'I' statement. So, instead of ranting at them, I stated my position, using the word 'I', and without apportioning blame. It sounded like this: 'When I come home, I am tired and need a tidy, peaceful space to sit and relax before I have to get on with the next job. When I come in and there are plates, clothes and other things all around the room, I can't relax and I get annoyed and frustrated, then I begin to feel unappreciated and I take it out on you. I don't like doing this and it would really help me if you came home and put your stuff upstairs, so that the living room is clear for me to come in and relax for a while.'

Some of our patterns we model from those around us and some are early instinctive behaviours. Either way, these behaviours get stuck as a pattern that we keep repeating, even though some of them do not work for us and do not get us what we need.

So many of our patterns are triggered by emotions. We think we are responding to the behaviour of others but, when our buttons get pressed, we are usually responding to our emotions, to what we want, need and feel.

So sometimes we are not aware we have a choice about the way we behave, we are simply responding to an old pattern, often one that was developed before we were three years old. This is why so many of us still have tantrums, and sulks, and why we say things to those we love in the heat of the moment that we later regret.

These old patterns are stored in the limbic part of the brain, where our unconscious competence is built. However, the behaviour we used to get our own way when we were two years old may need reprogramming, and some of the negative beliefs we have stored in there may also need to be reconsidered.

The next chapter about the limbic system shows how we can change old beliefs and patterns that no longer serve us.

SELF-CONTROL

NAME FEELINGS

DEALING WITH CONFLICT

Chapter 4

The limbic system

 If we are to reach real peace in this world ... We shall have to begin with the children.

Gandhi

How the limbic system affects our behaviour

 We cannot escape fear. We can only transform it into a companion that accompanies us on all our exciting adventures ... Take a risk a day – one small or bold stroke that will make you feel great once you have done it.

Susan Jeffers

The limbic system within the brain is where we record our emotional memory; the actual emotional response happens throughout the body. There is scientific evidence that shows emotions cause peptides to be released and there are receptors for these peptides in every part of the body. Therefore the emotions have a variety of effects on different areas within the body. When we experience fear, for example, we often feel it in our stomach, throat, knees, legs, hands, heart and so on.

> For a long time, neuroscientists have agreed that emotions are controlled by certain parts of the brain. This is a big, 'neurocentric' assumption – and I now think it is a wrong (or at least incomplete) one! ... In fact, the way in which peptides circulate through the body, finding their target receptors in regions far more distant than has ever previously been thought possible, made the brain communication system resemble the endocrine system, whose hormones can travel the length and breadth of our bodies ... One extremely important purpose of emotions, from an evolutionary perspective, is to help us decide what to remember and what to forget: The cave woman who could remember which cave had the gentle guy who gave her food is more likely to be our foremother, than the one who confused it with the cave that held the killer bear. The emotion of love (or something resembling it) and the emotion of fear would help secure her memories. Clearly, just as drugs can affect what we remember, neuropeptides can

> act as internal ligands to shape our memories as we are forming them and put us
> back in the same frame of mind when we need to retrieve them. This is learning.
> In fact we have shown that the hippocampus of the brain, without which we
> cannot learn anything new, is a nodal point for neuropeptide receptors,
> containing virtually all of them.
>
> Candace Pert[1]

To enable us to survive, the body has developed a very clever reaction within the limbic system. The two parts of the limbic system that control this reaction are the amygdala, a small almond-shaped structure in the middle of the limbic area, and the hippocampus, which is essential to recording experiences in memory.

In her book *Spiritual Intelligence,* Danah Zohar[2] describes the link between these two parts as 'associative thinking'. This kind of thinking allows us to form associations, for example, between hunger and the food that will satisfy it, between a mother's face and the feeling of love, between the sight of a spider and fear. It also allows for patterns such as the leap for joy when you see a certain face and linking together a group of skills like riding a bike or driving a car.

Because of the link between the sensory memory and the emotional memory, the brain is able to connect certain external experiences with a particular emotion. The brain does this even if the present experience is not quite the same as one in the past. It performs what is sometimes called a best fit. For example, a friend of mine has a strong fear of wasps; her pattern of behaviour whenever there is a wasp around is flight, and she runs as if her life were in real danger. Recently while driving her car in the fast lane of the motorway she heard a sound in her car that she registered as a wasp. The next thing she remembers is running up the hard shoulder of the motorway.

> It is not because things are difficult that we do not dare; it is because we do not dare that they are difficult.
>
> **Seneca**

Let us examine this reaction. First, the sound was not a wasp, but the brain did the best fit where buzz = wasp. Second, she risked her life and the lives of others by driving across two lanes of the motorway, throwing open her car door and running up the hard shoulder. Her brain was not using rational thinking, it was using associative thinking, which in this case linked the sound memory to fear, causing the release of adrenaline and a flight pattern of behaviour.

One of the amygdala's functions is to remember and connect memories of fear: events that have caused us to fight, flight, flock or freeze. As Pert[1] points out, the cave woman who did not associate a particular cave with the feeling of fear would not have survived very long.

In the brain, the hippocampus and the amygdala work together to enable us to respond very quickly to perceived danger. If a deer hears a crack in the distance, it does not wait to confirm what has caused the noise. It has learned that sound means danger, and the response in its brain is: crack (hippocampus remembers), fear (amygdala remembers). The reaction has become automatic and the deer runs. In some animals the response may be to fight or freeze. Each animal will have learned a response that worked in a previous situation, and so now performs it automatically. It will often have learned this from its parent.

This reaction is also true of humans. As animals we have the same response mechanisms in our brain, the same instinct for survival and the same reactions to fear. The fight, flight, flock or freeze response is automatic in us as well.

Many people say that this response is one of the reasons that prevents us from evolving. So often it is this response that traps us and causes us to push away and fight with those we love. Some would ask 'how can we have peace in the world when we have not got peace in our homes?' If we were always able to think consciously before we said or did anything, we could weigh up the short- and long-term results of our actions and choose well.

However, at the moment, for most people fear remains the cause of so much damaging behaviour because we are still allowing the limbic system to run some of the most important moments and make some of the most important choices of our lives. It could be said that we are permitting a primitive, instinctive response to fear to override our choice to love.

Emotional Intelligence gives us a way to break these old patterns and change our behaviour. It is an evolutionary step that we could choose to take, and it would need what some people call 'slow thinking': the ability to stop and think before reacting.

The effects of the limbic system on teaching and learning

Where did we ever get the crazy idea that to make people do better, first we have to make them feel worse? People do better when they feel better.

Jane Nelson

Now let us consider the effect that the limbic system has on teachers and pupils.

The following exercise will enable you to look at the behaviour patterns you have that you feel are not successful, the things you do and the reactions you have in response to certain behaviours.

Exercise

To enable you to really understand this essential part of Emotional Intelligence you will need to do this exercise and not just read it through.

Part 1 Think of a behaviour, something that the children or a child does that presses your buttons. This means that you react, you feel the reaction inside, you do not like what they are doing and the way you react is not successful.

Write down the following:

✿ Exactly what do they do, what is their behaviour?

✿ What do you think they are thinking and feeling when they do that?

✿ What do they need or want when they do that?

Take a look at your answers so far. Have you described their behaviour using words like annoying, rude, selfish, disrespectful, impatient, or any words that are judgements rather than actual behaviours? Or have you been able to describe their behaviour without judgement? For example, 'Starts to talk while someone else is still talking.'

Have you been able to really empathise with the children/child and think how they might be feeling or what they might need?

Part 2 When the children/child make that behaviour, how do you feel and what do you think?

✿ How do you respond, react, what do you do?

✿ What do you need or want at that time?

Again take a look at your answers and then ask yourself the questions in Part 3.

Part 3 ✿ Do you think you get what you really want or need in these situations?

✿ Do you think the children/child get what they really want or need from the situation?

✿ Look at what they are feeling. Do your feelings and reactions make sense? Do you normally react like that towards people who are feeling this way?

✿ Do you think you might be reacting more to your feelings or thoughts than you are to their behaviour, even though you may not like their behaviour?

Case study: a class teacher's story

A behaviour that really pressed one teacher's buttons was when a child looked up to the ceiling while being 'told off.' As we went through the above exercise, she initially described the behaviour as insolent and rude. She said the child was thinking 'I'll show you' and was feeling smug and wanted to show up the teacher, making her look stupid.

After discussing it with the group, she changed her mind and described the behaviour as it was – a child looking up at the ceiling and putting a particular expression on their face. She decided the child probably felt fear, embarrassment, humiliation and anger, and what they wanted was for her to stop and go away, or to be spoken to in a way that did not make them feel so humiliated. The child's pattern in this case is probably connected to the tone in the teacher's voice and the brain associates it with a feeling, for example, humiliation. This will cause a fear reaction, as most humans fear humiliation, and the child will have a response, in this case a flight reaction – look up to the ceiling and hope it will all go away.

When the teacher described her own feelings she was angry, even enraged, and also humiliated. She reacted to the situation by getting angrier and telling off the child in a tone that became more and more angry. What she wanted was for the child to look at her, listen to her and show her respect. But the more her tone changed, the more the child looked away, smiled and made faces. The more the child did this, the angrier she became.

What these two people wanted was to be treated with respect, to be listened to and to feel they were OK. When she looked truthfully at the situation, she did not feel she had treated the child with respect and said if the Head had spoken to her that way in front of everyone, she would have felt really humiliated, even if she had done something foolish.

She talked quite a lot about the way she would want to be given feedback about something she had not done well, or something that had upset someone. When she came to answer the questions in part 3 of the exercise, she said:

- ❀ 'No, I don't get what I need. I want to be treated with respect and I don't feel I get that.'

- ❀ 'No, the child does not get what they want either. They too want to be treated with respect and they don't feel that they are.'

- ❀ 'When people around me are feeling fearful, embarrassed or humiliated, no I don't normally feel anger, or rage.'

- ❀ 'Yes, I think I am reacting to my feelings, and my thoughts are adding fuel to the fire. I keep thinking things about the child – how rude they are and how dare they – that just makes me even angrier.'

Next she was asked, 'What do you think is the trigger – the thing that presses the button in the first place? Does it have any connection with fear?' She thought about it for a while and said, 'I think maybe deep down I'm always afraid when I have to confront someone for doing something I don't like. So, yes, I probably do feel some fear even before I start – fear that they won't listen, fear that I'll be shown up in front of all the other children, fear that they may just tell me where to go.' She went on to say that she had never really admitted that to herself before.

If after completing the above exercise you have come to any similar conclusions, if you can see that in this situation your response is not helping, it is not getting you what you want, yet you keep on doing it, then the response is automatic. Your amygdala is taking over and you may well be doing your version of fight, flight, flock or freeze. Alternatively, you may be performing some other pattern of behaviour that you have used before. It can be smiling sweetly and trying to be nice, or playing the clown and making light of it, but it will be an automatic response – what you always do to cover up or deal with your fear.

For young children in a school situation there is often much to fear. They frequently feel that they are not good enough, they are different, they do not fit in, they cannot get it right, or everyone else seems to know what to do and they do not. These and many other beliefs become who they are (their identity). They have statements running through their minds like 'I'm stupid', 'I'm not good enough', and so they are always trying to fit in, belong or get it right. This is how many of our amygdala responses develop. The fear of getting it wrong and not belonging has caused behaviour patterns to build up. Such patterns begin in childhood and our brain just goes on doing them forever unless we break the habit.

> If the only tools you have are hammers every problem begins to look like a nail.
>
> **Abraham Maslow**

Current knowledge suggests that inside the brain the limbic system and the reptilian function, also called the brain stem, work together when fear is registered. The reptilian part of the brain is responsible for survival: it controls heartbeat and other survival functions, and regulates the release of adrenaline. In less than a second fear can be registered in the amygdala, the reptilian function sends a message to the adrenals, adrenaline is released, the heart speeds up, the liver releases glucose and the muscles get ready to run or fight.

The neo-cortex is the part of the brain where our conscious thinking takes place. This part seems to work much more slowly than the limbic system and the reptilian function. Current knowledge shows that the amygdala and hippocampus recognises some small memory: a tone in someone's voice, a look, the mention of a spelling test. The amygdala remembers fear, which can be as real to the body as a man-eating tiger in the room. The reptilian function then acts and instantly causes the body to prepare. The automatic response will be something that has been patterned in and seems to get us out of danger. If smiling will protect us, we smile, even if we are terrified.

While this has happened the neo-cortex is not engaged; we are not consciously thinking. This is why if you ask someone after an amygdala response why they acted as they did, they cannot tell you.

Children who have been abused often have a form of freeze as a response. They are not able to fight or run so they shut down, go inside and close off the world. It is a means of survival. There are many forms of abuse and not all of them are immediately obvious. Yet the results can be similar: every time the person feels fear in later life, whether the fear is real or imagined, the body will react. The shut down happening inside and closing off the world is a response that is common in many adults.

As humans we have learned a wide variety of responses to protect ourselves. Many of these we modelled from the adults around us when we were young. Whenever we feel under threat, we automatically respond. Often it is fear responses that cause problems in school. Children will perform their version of the fight, flight, flock or freeze. School is not a very safe place for many children or adults, and so we see a lot of automatic, amygdala responses there, from both the children and the adults.

Changing behaviour patterns

 Take your life in you own hands and what happens? A terrible thing: no one to blame.

Erica Jong

Actions

If we want less automatic fight, flight, freeze, flock responses in our classrooms, then the fear levels need to come down and children and adults need to feel safe. Stress is a major factor in these responses. Adults are more likely to snap and respond with anger when they are stressed, and it is the same for children. The first action we can take to support children to move beyond their automatic behaviour is to work at breaking our own patterns of automatic behaviour. While we respond to our buttons being pressed, and our behaviour is heated and annoyed, the tension in a room is heightened. This makes it very difficult, if not impossible, for children's responses to be anything different from those their brain has already set up to do to protect them.

If we can break some of our patterns, we will learn how it is done and then we can teach the children how to do it. While we are working on our own patterns we can show children how we are doing it, explain how it works, or does not, and how we are practising and becoming more capable at it. Consider the following:

❖ Make your school a much safer place to be by recognising the triggers that cause particular children to respond in a way that is obviously automatic. We can make the system less threating by following the actions listed below.

❖ Teach the children about the amygdala response so that they understand what is happening to them and can work with you to break the pattern.

❖ Teach yourself and the children 'slow thinking' – think before you speak or act.

❖ Connect with all the children in your care and help them to feel they belong. Much of their fear comes from a sense of being outside and not fitting in.

❖ Work on self-esteem and self-concept.

❖ Work on negative self-talk and developing optimism.

❖ Teach children how to change their emotional state whenever they need so they are not at the mercy of their emotions and their responses to them.

grow, grow

❖ Teach children how to go beyond the confines of the personality/identity they seem to have been given by the world around them (for example, the naughty boy, the bully, the shy one, the bossy one). Enable them to create an identity that grows as they grow and is more in keeping with who they want to be.

❖ Support children through the first stages of belonging and taking on the values and beliefs of the group to the stage where they begin to look at, question and develop their own.

❖ Teach ourselves to do all these things, so that we can model them and teach them to children.

All these areas will be covered later in the book, but here I want to place them in the context of changing behaviour patterns. When we are looking at these patterns, it often feels as though the other person's behaviour is the trigger to our response; however, it is our interpretation of their behaviour that is really the trigger. The associations we make in our brain are what we respond to. If a child looks up at the ceiling and our association is disrespect, the feelings linked with that will probably be fear based and we will have an automatic response. If, however, we associate it with a child feeling embarrassed, we will not feel threatened and we will have a different response. Being able to manage our feelings and responses is the first part of Emotional Intelligence.

> Every blade of grass has an Angel that bends over it and whispers, 'Grow, grow.'
>
> **The Talmud**

Breaking the pattern/choosing our response

 A journey of a thousand miles begins with a single step.
Lao-Tzu

One way of learning how to break your pattern is to choose a pattern that repeats quite often – one you would really wish to break.

Parents sometimes select a repeating pattern they have with their children. A common example is when children get ready for school in the morning and the parent reaches a point where they 'lose it'. The situation ends with children and parent going their different ways, upset and hurt.

One mother recently walked into work looking upset and angry, she said, 'I can't believe what I ended up saying to my son this morning, I'm such a b****.' How familiar that sounds to all of us; we have all done it with someone. What effect might this have on her relationship with her 12-year-old son? Particularly as it is not just a one-off but a repeating pattern that happens most mornings.

Another example teachers sometimes choose is coming back to their class after another teacher has taken it, or after the lunch-time break. They return to hear a list of complaints about the dreadful way that the children behaved. The teacher is often triggered before even entering the classroom. The button has already been pressed and the angry tirade of disappointment, anger and blame begins. Some teachers have this button pressed continuously and their enjoyment of their job and of the children with whom they work is seriously damaged.

When you have chosen a pattern you would like to work on, you need to start recognising the signals that come just before your button gets pressed. Go through the events in your mind or do it with a friend. Find that moment when you know you will blow but you are still in control. Detecting the point before the amygdala has taken over is very important.

Now you have a choice of things you can try. These might include:

* preparing a thought that you could implant at that moment, one that would cause you to ponder, laugh or smile. In fact any thought that does not create an angry, guilty or fearful response. This thought needs to be six seconds or longer to override the amygdala and the automatic/patterned response.

* using the exercise on page 42 to think about how the other person is feeling right now and what they want right now. This focus uses the neo-cortex and enables the effects of the amygdala to be overridden.

* thinking of something you love about your children, or remembering the last great time you had together, or the next good time you want to have together.

Recently a group of mothers who found their children's untidy bedrooms to be a big 'button pusher' changed their reaction. A woman whose child had been killed at the age of 14 spoke to them about how much she missed her daughter's messy bedroom. Now every time these mothers look into their child's messy bedroom they feel grateful.

Using 'I' statements

 Most problems cannot be solved at the level at which they are asked.
Zen Koan

Another valuable method for breaking patterns is using 'I' statements (see page 160). Here the focus is on the outcome: what I want to get from the next reaction I have with the children (or with anyone), how can I say what I feel and say what I need with total respect for the other person and remembering that they also have feelings and needs, which may clash with mine.

'I' statements work in the following way:

1   You state the behaviour *you* find difficult.
2   You state the effect it is having on *you* or from *your* perspective.
3   You state how *you* are feeling.
4   You state what *you* need.

The mother who has the morning difficulty could use 'I' statements as follows:

1   When you get up late and are not ready to go when I am …
2   I get very stressed because I fear I will be late for work, or I will have to leave you here and then you will be late for school, and you will get detention and I will be called in. It is affecting our relationship because the mornings feel so stressful.
3   I feel really angry, frustrated and upset.
4   I need you to be responsible for getting yourself to school on time, either by leaving with me or by some other means. I want to enjoy my time with you in the mornings so we can part with a smile.

To be Emotionally Intelligent you need to understand how the above experience is working, why it is effecting a change, why 'I' statements give us more power in our personal responses and what effect they have on the children. When we understand how and why they work, we can use them repeatedly to break patterns that do not work well for us, choose responses and communicate effectively. We can also support children to do the same.

How 'I' statements work

1   While using 'I' statements the neo-cortex is engaged and you are thinking consciously about the words you are going to use. This prevents the amygdala from taking over.

2   You are modelling the behaviour that we all need to learn – how we tell people about how we feel and what we need so that they can really understand and do not feel blamed, bad, wrong or confused.

3   You are helping children to learn empathy skills.

4   You are helping children to connect behaviour, and the outcomes of their behaviour, without damaging their self-esteem.

5   You are not damaging your relationship with the child.

6   You are far less stressed as you are producing less adrenaline.

7   You are showing the child or person you love them and that your relationship with them is important.

Helping children in the classroom

 I hear and I forget.
I see and I remember.
I do and I understand.

Chinese proverb

To support children or anyone to change a behaviour pattern that is not working well for them (that is, they realise that the long-term effects are not what they want), then the following method has been used with success.

Stage one: ABC

The first step is either to support the child, young person or adult to carry out the ABC method or to observe and do it ourselves. The method covers the following stages:

Antecedence	What was happening before the behaviour?
	How were you feeling?
	What were you thinking and doing?
	What did you want?
	What was your mood?
	Had someone just upset you?
Behaviour	What actually happened? – the facts
	What did you do and say?
	What did the other person or people do or say?
Consequences	What was the result of the behaviour? – long-term and short-term consequences

This method enables patterns to be established. Sometimes the antecedence is the key – the person is usually in a hurry, or feeling pressured or stressed. Or the behaviour can give the clue – maybe someone looks at the person in a certain way, or it is the tone in their voice.

The consequences allow you to see and discuss what the person might be getting out of the behaviour in the short term and, in the long term, whether it is really serving them. How does it match with their values and aspirations? For example, when talking to a child about the long-term consequences of losing their temper, they generally realise that it will affect how their friends see them and whether they are invited to parties (no one wants someone at their party who might flare up and lose control). Being invited to parties might be very important to them – something they value – and this can become the reason they will work with you to change the pattern.

Stage two

Recognising the pattern is often very effective and both adults and children usually understand that when they have been upset or annoyed by one person, the next person to come along may well have all the anger or tears unloaded on them.

Many years ago I spent some time with prison officers, who have a very difficult and stressful job. At one point in the discussion I asked them, 'What do you do with all that anger?' (They were very heated at the time, describing what they had to handle.) Their replies were honest and moved me deeply. One man became very tearful and said, 'I go home and dump it all over my wife and kids.' At that time (and maybe still) officers had no support with the very strong, deep emotional responses they were dealing with.

Adults do this all the time. We come in from a hard day, or a traffic jam, and all it takes is for someone to look at us the wrong way and we explode. If we want to break the pattern, we need to do something to release the feeling – scream in the car, walk in the park, kick a ball around, play squash, have a relaxing swim. Many people know that they cannot go straight home and some go to the pub or sports club. These people have recognised that the antecedence to their behaviour when they arrive home is due to stressful, angry feelings they have built up during the day. Some people are in jobs where they cannot release that level of anger and need to find a healthy way of freeing it that does not damage others.

If the difficulty seems to arise from the behaviour section, it is usually easy to find out what is triggering it. A child or an adult will generally blame someone else for the outburst of anger. Use the pattern breaking exercise to enable them to separate the other person's pattern from theirs. Find out what the person thinks about the other's behaviour. Sometimes they have decided that a smile is disrespectful, or sarcastic; often the reason for a reaction is not what the other person does but why we think they did it.

Some of the language work on optimism in Chapter 11 will be helpful in changing people's perceptions. For example, a Year 3 child once came to me feeling bullied, she explained Mary was looking at her. When I asked her to tell me a bit more she said, 'Every time I look up in class she is looking at me. She does it in the playground. She hates me.'

I asked, 'What if she is looking at you because she likes you?' The child looked puzzled, and so I just said, 'Go back to class and every time she looks at you think to yourself "she's looking at me because she likes me" and see what happens.' The child came back to me the next day and said, 'You're right. She wanted to be my friend.'

All that happened was the child changed her thought. When we change our thoughts our actions automatically change, it is one of the psychological laws. When she saw the girl looking and thought 'she likes me', it caused her to smile. The other girl smiled back and a friendship started.

Another way of effecting change in behaviour is the use of 'I' statements. As I stated earlier, 'I' statements are a true communication from one person to another; they do not blame or judge and so they do not usually cause a defensive response. People can often hear them without its triggering their own insecurities.

If the area you need to focus on is the consequences, then the exercise on short- and long-term consequences in the intrinsic motivation section (activity page 172) will be helpful. The link here is values and aspirations, which are covered fully in later chapters. I used this with Joe (see pages 16–18) to begin the process of change that helped him alter his thoughts and feelings.

Chapter 5

Fear and love

Is love an emotion? This is a question that has been asked by numerous people and religions. Many spiritual teachers will say that love is the essence of who we are and in our completely natural untouched state we would just be unconditional love.

This spiritual vision of human nature has prevailed against all the odds. Its roots go back in India more than two thousand years to the Vedic scriptures. The Vedas say that it is much more natural for us to create from love than from non-love. They declare that humans 'are born in bliss, sustained in bliss and return to bliss again after death'. This is a drastic shift in perception from modern psychology ... to have a complete vision of love means being willing to undergo a much more total shift of perception. When you perceive yourself as spirit, you will not simply feel love – you will be love.

In spiritual terms, to be love is only natural. It is our departure from love that is unnatural.

Deepak Chopra[1]

I have discussed the amygdala reaction and how it is programmed to respond to fear. Fear causes us to fight, fly, freeze or flock. All of them have helped us to survive, but these patterned responses also close us down and take us away from people, away from being in relationships.

> Love is that which is unlimited. There is no beginning and no end to it ... You will find that you always seek to love, and to be loved ... A child experiences no fear. He thinks he can do anything. Nor does a child experience lack of freedom. She thinks she can love anyone. Nor does a child experience lack of life ... nor does a child know ungodly things – until that child is taught ungodly things by grownups. And so, children run around naked and hug everyone, thinking nothing of it. If adults could only do the same thing.
>
> Neale Donald Walsch[2]

In his book *Emotional Intelligence*, Daniel Goleman[3] gives an example of a man walking by a canal. The man sees a woman standing looking into the canal with a shocked expression on her face. The next thing the man knows he is in the canal and saving a small child from drowning. Goleman uses this as an example of an instinctive reaction, and it begs the question, 'Did the act stem from love or fear?'

People perform the most amazing acts of heroism; there are even programmes on television dedicated to them. People leap into freezing water, jump into lions' cages to rescue a child, walk into burning buildings to save people. If fear was the predominant emotion in those cases, they would run away or freeze. During wars and times of natural disaster countless people risk their own lives to save others, often complete strangers.

 Live with great expectations, and great things happen.
Art Fettig

This could be evidence that humans are naturally inclined to love; our basic urge is to show love, and we see evidence of this all the time. It is only when we allow fear to get in the way of love that our natural responses change.

If there is some area of your life that is not working well and you find yourself complaining about it, the following strategy may help.

A teacher was complaining about her class for months: no one understood how difficult they were, no one supported her, the children were not punished enough, they were getting away with everything, no one gave a damn about her ... and so on.

I asked her what she was getting from continuously complaining about her class. She did not like the question. You may not like the question either, but it is a useful one to ask yourself. It took some time and some help for her to realise what she was getting out of complaining:

❀ Blaming other people, so it was not her fault.

❀ Getting a lot of people to feel sorry for her.

- Getting a lot of people to agree with her about how dreadful the children were.

- Getting people to agree with her about how unsupportive the Head was.

- Feeling like the poor victim at the mercy of these terrible children.

- Being in the right; she was the 'goody' and they were the 'baddies'.

- Not having to change anything she did.

- Not even having to consider changing.

I then asked her what did she lose by complaining all the time – what was the cost? She did not like that question either. Again it took some time for her to realise it:

- No one could help her or really support her while she insisted on being a victim.

- She had completely forgotten how much she really liked and cared for the children she taught.

- The children had to be in the room with a miserable, angry woman every day for months and so had forgotten how much they really liked her too.

- All the fun and enjoyment had gone out of the job.

- Other adults in the school were finding her hard to be around and so avoided her.

- This really wonderful person was missing and no one could reach her.

- No one could offer her honest feedback about how they felt around her.

- Any support that might have helped was not offered as there was no point.

When love goes missing, we lose the chance to really love the children and they do not get a chance to love us in return. Usually when we complain a lot about something, we are being the victim, and victims cause others around them to either rescue or persecute them.

> Man is asked to make of himself what he is supposed to become to fulfil his destiny.
>
> **Paul Tillich**

Generally people try to rescue victims first (but this is never possible), then when they get nowhere, due to the 'yes buts' or the 'but this is different' or 'you have no idea what it is like', they become frustrated or angry with the victim and thus turn into a persecutor.

Victims act from fear not love; fear takes over and runs their lives. When we are in the victim role, we are stuck or frozen. Fear of taking responsibility for changing things in our lives causes us just to complain about them instead.

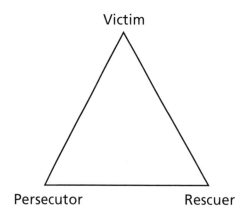

A victim

1 Complains but does not take action.

2 Asks for advice, then says 'Yes but ....'

3 Says, 'Fix me. Make me better.'

4 Says, 'It's not fair', 'You're so lucky', 'If only ....'

5 Is a frustrator who leaves you feeling helpless and impotent.

6 Avoids the struggle to be herself, colludes with the oppressor, will not assert power.

7 Has shame and helplessness as dominant emotions.

Each time we complain and do nothing about it, we are in the victim role. Someone or something is doing it to us. We are denying our power to be in control of our own lives. It can be a very difficult at times to remember that how we receive, and react to, events in our lives is within our power. There are stories of people who were in camps during the Second World War and refused to be victims. Within themselves they were able to use their terrible experiences to grow as people. Some of them used these experiences to learn forgiveness and were capable of true forgiveness for the people imprisoning them. Some believed that the cost to the Nazis, in terms of what they were doing and what they would have to live with, was far greater than the physical cost to themselves. Because they refused to blame and saw their persecutors as victims, they were, within themselves, free.

> One of the most moving love stories I've ever read happened between two enemies in the holocaust. A devout Catholic was suffering in a hideous medical 'experiment' being conducted at Auschwitz. She was a young woman, and as it happened the doctor who presided over her clinical torture was also a woman, which somehow made the sadism all the more horrifying. Death came slowly, but at last it came. The young woman whispered intelligibly, and the doctor, assuming she was uttering a curse, drew back. The young woman reached out. She struggled to lift something from her neck and managed to hold it out to her tormentor, 'for you' she was whispering as she handed her rosary to the doctor, a last blessing as she departed the world.
>
> Deepak Chopra[1]

These people are exceptional, most of us can go into victim role if we pick the wrong queue at the supermarket – 'It's not fair!' or 'Why do I always get the trainee cashier?' are very common reactions. The key to whether you become a victim or not is in the emotional response you have to the situation, and often the key to the emotional response is the internal dialogue you are playing in your head, or the patterns of behaviour based on fear you have developed.

> It is difficult to make a man miserable while he feels worthy of himself and claims kindred to the great God who made him.
>
> **Abraham Lincoln**

Many teachers have become victims: they are victims of the system. As a teacher myself I often found myself in this trap and the following strategy was, and is, very helpful.

Question: If you could give the children in your care one guaranteed gift or quality, by the time they left you, what would that be?

There is usually a range of responses to this question, but the following three are always the most common: self-confidence, self-esteem, and respect for themselves and others. If I were to spend a week in your classroom, would I know from what I see, hear and feel, that this is what you believe is most important? Do you teach in such a way that every interaction raises self-esteem, or do you plan and prepare lessons so that all children build self-confidence?

Some people say that they consciously plan for this, as if it were the most important thing to them. However, most people go immediately into victim role and blame the literacy hour, numeracy hour, OFSTED, the National Curriculum, pressures from above, and from outside. Within two to three minutes a whole group can become victims and create a group victim mentality. This is the reason why people then feel powerless. Victims cause you to become victims with them, or become rescuers or persecutors – unless you are able to be Emotionally Intelligent about what is happening.

In this situation, teachers know they are not being true to what they believe, they know that the way they provide learning for the pupils does not suit everyone in the room. They know that often they are damaging self-confidence, self-esteem and self-respect. This is why morale among teachers can be very low – they are not behaving in a way that is true to their values.

> The pearl is hid in the field, and the field is in the world and the world is in your heart, and there you must dig deep to find it, and when you have digged deep and found it, you must sell all to purchase and redeem this field.
>
> **George Fox**

Going into victim role is a fear reaction, and means you can complain but do not have to put yourself on the line. Teachers who become victims complain about the system, the children and their behaviour, the parents and how they bring up their children, the Head.

Not all teachers go into victim role; some do what they believe will develop the children's self-confidence, self-esteem and self-respect. They do it regardless of the system, or the behaviour of the children or parents; they do it because that is more important to them than anything else.

A persecutor

1   Is isolated.

2   Is critical and aggressive (this can be active or passive aggression).

3   Is rigid, fixed, defines things in black and white.

4   Enjoys fighting as a way of staying distant and not showing vulnerability.

5   Fears that if boundaries soften, they will not exist (fear of intimacy).

6   Will give up everything to be right.

7   Projects hostility/negativity/anger onto others to justify defensive behaviour.

8   Feels justified in their persecution.

9   Puts out 'go away' and 'I don't need you' messages.

10   Has anger as dominant emotion.

When we are being right at any cost, including in our relationships, we are in persecutor role. This usually happens in response to an amygdala reaction. For example, if your partner does not phone, or he arrives and there is a certain look on his face, or a certain tone in his voice, you can find yourself in a fear reaction. If you then have a fight reaction (fight, flight, freeze), you will become angry and begin to fight him. He will be standing there wondering what is going on, and you will continue being angry pushing him away with your words or actions, even though you love him and he has done nothing. If you stay in persecutor role, you will keep it up despite knowing you are seriously damaging your relationship. Being right becomes more important than friendship, love, or the relationship.

You may have found yourself on the receiving end of this and been at a loss to know what to do. No matter how much you try to explain, persecutor will not listen because they have to make you wrong in order to be right.

> Tolerance is not concession, not indifference. Tolerance is the knowledge of others. It is mutual respect through mutual understanding. Let's throw out the old myths and take up the results of current research. Man is not violent by nature. Intolerance is not 'in our genes'. Fear and ignorance are the root causes of intolerance, and its patterns can be imprinted on the human psyche from an early age.
>
> Federico Mayor (Director-General of UNESCO)[4]

A rescuer

1   Avoids conflict and desires harmony.

2   Deprives others of resources (disempowers).

3   Attends to the needs of others (compulsive responder) and neglects own needs.

4   Is seen as good, warm, caring.

5   Is someone who can easily adapt.

6 Seeks to take the pain away (steals their experience). Underlying message: 'Don't have this experience – you aren't big enough to cope with it/I can't handle seeing you in pain.'

7 Projects sadness, seeks and imagines sadness in others (overly sympathetic).

8 Has difficulty saying no and maintaining boundaries.

9 Gives 'come to me' messages, 'I will save you/help you/do it for you/I really understand you.'

10 Has guilt as the dominant emotion – feels overly responsible for everything.

We often go into rescuer role when we are concerned about and cannot cope with other people's emotions, but it is really our own sense of guilt and responsibility that we fear. It is easier to be nice and appease people than it is to be honest and tell them in 'I statements' (see page 160) how they are affecting you.

These three roles form the triangle we act in a lot of the time. In simple terms, when we are complaining about things we are in victim role, when we are critical and blaming we are in persecutor role, and when we do not speak our truth because it might upset someone or we might be rejected, we are in rescuer role. All these roles devolve from a basis of fear not love, even though many of us believe we are being loving when we rescue people.

When the teacher is complaining, she is being a victim: it is all happening to her, she has no control over it. If someone tries to rescue her, she stays in victim role and frustrates the person until they start to feel very critical and annoyed and become the persecutor; or she stays in victim role and attracts other victims, who all sit and moan together about how dreadful it is, how unfair it is, and how it is being done to them; or, lastly, she stays in victim role, gets angry with the rescuer, blames him, and then changes role for a while and becomes the persecutor.

Very small children have not usually learned these roles. They acquire such roles by imitation from the adults around them and are also affected by the roles in a very profound way.

The effects the roles have on children

PARENT/ADULT		CHILD WILL FEEL
Victim	⟶	Guilt, anger, powerless
Persecutor	⟶	Powerless, anger, guilt
Rescuer	⟶	Powerless, anger, guilt

Which of these three roles children adopt depends on other factors, like how they perceive themselves within the family and within the school.

If we wish to escape this triangle and behave in a way that is Emotionally Intelligent, then we need to be able to say how it is for us without blame or complaint; and others need to be able to say how it is for them without being blamed, responsible, or attacked. Levellers are able to do this. A leveller can state how things are for them without blaming, can be sensitive and caring without placating or going into agreement and does not wear a mask

A leveller

1   Is able to distance herself but still be in touch with feelings.

2   Is able to stay with her own centre and act in line with her values.

3   Is honest and authentic in communications.

4   Informs others about her own needs, wants, emotions, desires and visions.

5   Is flexible, not fixed.

6   Maintains a sense of self even though the price may be rejection.

7   Asserts self without overpowering others.

Guidelines for levelling

1   Do not pressure yourself to respond. Remember you do not have to decide, talk, fix, hug, smile or advise until you are ready and on solid ground.

2   Do not respond on impulse. Check where you are coming from. Do not impulsively agree to requests.

3   Make your goal 'I'm OK, you're OK, even thought we both have problems'.

4   Ask permission to deal with issues (avoids disempowering others).

5   Be specific and clear about what you want.

6   Reinforce the other person's strengths.

7   Recognise when you begin to slip into persecutor, victim or rescuer role from your own posture, attitudes and responses, and learn to change or re-organise these roles.

8   Use 'I' statements to say how you feel and how you are being affected.

9   Remember you can always let go of your investment in playing these games. You can always change you, even though you cannot force someone else to change.

Life is no brief candle to me. It is a sort of splendid torch which I have got hold of for the moment, and I want to make it burn as brightly as possible before handing it on to future generations.

George Bernard Shaw

If one advances confidently in the direction of his dreams, and endeavours to live the life which he has imagined, he will meet with success unexpected in common hours.

Henry David Thoreau

To be able to follow the guidelines, children and adults need to:

- ❀ develop assertiveness skills
- ❀ increase, their sense of worth and self-esteem
- ❀ clarify their values and beliefs so that they can live consistently with them
- ❀ develop emotional literacy and emotional intelligence
- ❀ understand about relationships and respectful conflict resolution
- ❀ use 'I' statements.

When these skills and understandings are in place there is no need for us to be victims, persecutors or rescuers.

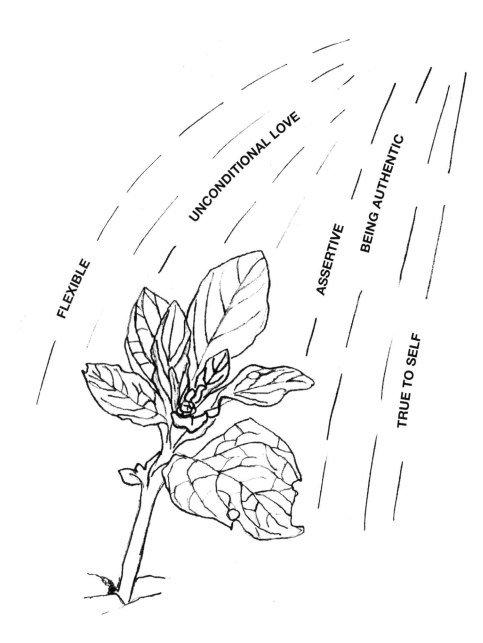

Chapter 6

The emotional effects of grief

 When you are sorrowful, look again in your heart, and you shall see that in truth you are weeping for that which has been your delight.

Khalil Gibran

Grief

Deep sobs –
That start beneath my heart
And hold my body in a grip that hurts.
The lump swells inside my throat
Brings pain that tries to choke.
Then tears course down my cheeks –
I drop my head in my so empty hands
Abandoning myself to deep dark grief
And know that with the passing time
Will come relief.
That though the pain may stay
There soon will come a day
When I can say her name and be at peace.

Norah Leney[1]

The experience of loss causes us to feel grief, and the depth of this emotion seems to be equal to the love, delight, joy and pleasure we have received. We experience loss from the moment we are born:

- ❀ The loss of the world of the womb, the separation from our mother's body.
- ❀ Going to school/nursery and being separated from parents.
- ❀ Change from nursery to school and loss of familiar surroundings and friends.
- ❀ New siblings, which can cause some loss of attention.

- ❀ Death of a sibling, which causes parents to be preoccupied and withdrawn, plus the loss of someone close.

- ❀ Moving to a new area, which may mean loss of friends, school and familiar environment.

- ❀ Loss of a grandparent, through death.

- ❀ Loss of a parent through separation, divorce or death.

- ❀ Older siblings moving away from home.

- ❀ Moving to a different country or culture.

- ❀ Finding out you have diabetes, or have to wear glasses or a hearing aid can result in a feeling of loss: loss of status, self-esteem, friends and participation in activities. The degree of loss will depend on a child's perception of the disability and the reaction of those close to him.

- ❀ Child sexual abuse – can result in a loss of innocence and self-esteem/worth.

- ❀ Hospital stay – can result in a loss of familiar surroundings.

These, and many more, losses can occur in children's lives while they are at school. The effect of these losses is some degree of grief. Grief is a natural emotion; it consists of many phases and causes us to experience many different feelings.

We cannot prevent the birds of sorrow from landing on our shoulder. We can prevent them from nesting in our hair.

Old Chinese proverb

Becoming Emotionally Intelligent – Catherine Corrie

Stages of grief

Stage one	Shock and disbelief	This happens to us when our model of the world is disrupted. Shock can take the form of physical pain or numbness. Children can become apathetic and withdrawn or abnormally calm. The numbness is a form of defence that enables us to cope. Occasionally shock takes the form of anger.
Stage two	Denial	This usually occurs within the first 14 days and can last minutes, hours or weeks. During this stage the person behaves as if there has been no loss and as though their circumstances have not changed.
Stage three	Growing awareness	During this stage the waves of feeling can become overwhelming. Waves of tears, anger, guilt, sadness and loneliness can come one after the other. The following feelings may be experienced in this stage:

During this stage the waves of feeling can become overwhelming. Waves of tears, anger, guilt, sadness and loneliness can come one after the other. The following feelings may be experienced in this stage:

❀ yearning and pining

❀ anger

❀ sadness

❀ guilt

❀ anxiety.

Stage four	Acceptance	This generally occurs about two years or more after a death or a major separation.

Sometimes children do not pass through the 'stages of grief' without getting stuck. They will then need support to enable them to work through the block and move forward through the grief process. Some of the blocks are as follows:

❀ refusing to accept the loss and not letting go

❀ not being prepared to allow themselves to grieve

❀ not really believing it

❀ having mixed feelings about the person who has gone

❀ not being allowed to attend funerals

❀ experiencing a succession of losses and no time to grieve

❀ things being left unsaid

❀ parents grieving so the child feels they cannot

❀ emotions being disapproved of by schools parents, so no place to express them.

There are three ways that children sometime cope with loss that are not helpful over a long period and need to be faced by the grieving child:

1   Substitution – the child may try to find a substitute mother or father.

2   Aggression – the child may be always fighting. A variety of discipline problems may occur both inside and outside school.

3   Helplessness – this leads to a lack of curiosity and so impedes learning. The child may opt out of life – even become deaf in extreme cases.

Dealing with the emotions

 Nothing in the world is as soft and yielding as water. Yet for dissolving the hard and inflexible, nothing can surpass it.

Tao Te Ching

Children often have difficulty working through and expressing sadness and anger, when past experiences have given them a fear of showing emotions around adults. They are usually not sure what is allowed; tears are sometime met with disapproval or discomfort from both adults and peers, 'Don't cry, you are a big boy/girl now' or 'Cry baby'. Tears can be the only way to heal the pain. They are a normal, natural response for releasing pain.

Anger

Anger!

Anger is black
Anger is red
Anger steams inside your head
Whirling round getting you mad
Getting you hotter, making you bad.

You feel you want to be evil
To every one you see
And hatred and horrible
Is all you want to be.

Anger gets you tight and tense
Your fists seem to tightly clench
You shout and scream and cry and howl
Then the anger's not there at all.

Sophie Stevens[2]

Most adults and children fear anger, so the child who is grieving does not feel allowed to express it.

Anger is felt as a surge of energy in one or more of these three areas:

- ❀ the mouth – bite, spit, scream or swear
- ❀ the hands – punch, hit, poke, break, pull
- ❀ the legs and feet – stamp, kick, trip, run.

The anger is frequently expressed indirectly, or projected on to someone or something. This is because it has been squashed down inside where it builds up into rage and guilt. The child will provoke those around her to get a reaction and this will allow her to vent her anger. If a child is angry with a parent for leaving, and yet at the same time loves the parent, she often feels guilty. She will not express the anger towards the parent but channels it indirectly towards anyone else she can provoke.

Aggressive behaviour

Aggressive behaviour grows from the feeling of helplessness that is often experienced in the early stages of loss. A child will become hostile towards adults and aggressive towards other children. In most cases this behaviour will change as the child moves through the stages of grief, but in a few it may persist as some need is being served by it.

There is a Knot

There is a knot inside of me
A knot which cannot be untied
Strong
It hurts
As if they have put a stone
Inside of me

I always remember the old days
Playing at our summer home
Going to Grandmother
Staying at Grandmother's

I want those days to return
Perhaps the knot will be untied
When they return
But there is a knot inside of me
So strong
And it hurts
As if there is a stone inside of me.

Translation of a poem by a Turkish Girl[3]

Guilt

Children will often ask themselves, 'What did I do to deserve this?' or 'What is wrong with me?' Their self-esteem is affected by the misplaced belief that there is something wrong with them. This guilt, if it is unconscious, can manifest itself as physical ailments, being accident prone, or making negative choices in relationships and other areas.

A child can also feel guilty because he believes the loss is due to 'wrong' feelings on his part. For example, he may have thought 'I wish you would disappear' or 'Go to Hell'. He may then deny any feelings at all, responding to the world in a very uncaring way, 'I don't care and you can't make me.' He is usually suffering from loss of concentration and confusion, and so learning, making decisions, setting goals or trusting his own experiences is very difficult. Such children will frequently say, 'I can't', 'I don't know' or 'it's too hard'.

Supporting children through the grief process

Teachers can support children through the grief process by allowing them to express the various emotions they have to go through.

Exercises that allow children to state how they feel today can be done every day. A simple exercise is to invite children to close their eyes and take their attention to their body. They check the different parts from toes to scalp and discover where there is any tension or which area attracts them. Then they try to put a name to the feeling they think is stored in that part. Ask them to focus on that part of their body and send it love. The physical release of anger has to be allowed in a safe and permitted way. If a child has a hitting feeling, they know they are not allowed to hit a person but they can hit a cushion, or a ball, or they can bang pieces of clay, or hammer in nails. When they have a kicking feeling, they are not allowed to kick a person but they can kick a ball, run around the field, or stamp their feet.

Adults are often afraid of anger because it is a very powerful release of energy. However, it is very important to respect the amount of energy there is present and allow it to be released safely. If children seem to be losing control, it is very important to support them, to say you can see it is becoming hard for them to stop and to suggest they sit and cool off. Support them to think of a memory of either a happy or fun time. This can allow the sense of managing themselves to return.

If a child is behaving aggressively, allow him to problem solve and think of solutions for dealing with the situation. This way he begins to feel more in control and less helpless.

How to help people suffering from loss

❀ Let your genuine concern and caring show.

❀ Be available – to listen or help with whatever else seems needed at the time.

❀ Say you are sorry about what happened and about their pain.

❀ Allow them to express as much unhappiness as they are feeling at the moment and are willing to share.

❀ Encourage them to be patient with themselves, not to expect too much of themselves and not to impose any 'shoulds' on themselves.

❀ Allow them to talk about their loss as much and as often as they want to.

❀ Talk about the special, endearing qualities of what they have lost.

❀ Reassure them that they did everything they could.

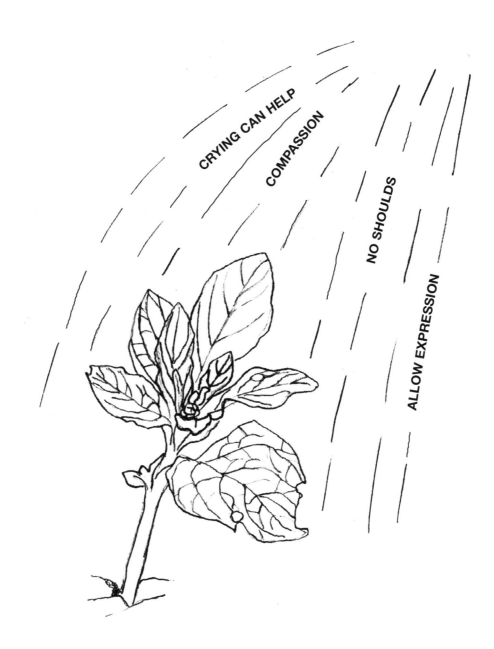

Chapter 7

Connecting with the children in our care

 If you judge people, you have no time to love them.

Mother Teresa

Everyone needs to belong

At the early stage of development, when belonging is crucial to a child's feeling of safety, one of the biggest gifts we can give them is to connect with them. This chapter examines what *exactly* is meant by connection and what it is that makes us feel comfortable with one person and not with another. The best way to discover how to connect is to examine, in detail, the reasons why you connect with some people in your life and not others. First, look at your place of work: are there some people with whom you feel a connection and some you do not? Imagine yourself with one of the people with whom you feel a connection and write down how it feels. Typical responses are:

- ❀ I can be myself.

- ❀ I don't feel judged.

- ❀ I can be vulnerable.

❀ I can be angry.

❀ I don't have to worry about what I say.

❀ It feels OK for us to not agree on everything.

❀ I can tell them how I feel, even when I'm afraid.

❀ They don't tell me what to do.

❀ I feel accepted.

❀ I feel I'm OK.

One of the most common causes of keeping our distance and not connecting with people is the feeling of being judged and, worse, of being judged as not OK – that there is something about us that needs fixing. In any personal relationship, no matter how close, as soon as we begin to feel not good enough and that the other person wants us to change, we begin to disconnect. Counsellors hear, time and time again, how successful relationships started to go wrong when one person began to find fault with the other and wanted them to change. Relate this to the children who work or live with us. How do we see them? How do we judge them?

Exercise (repeated from pages 25 and 27)

Try the following.

1 List the names of the children, or adults, you work with. If you are a class teacher, list the names of all the children in your class vertically, with a space beside each name.

a) How easy was it to remember all the names?

b) Which were the people you struggled to remember?

2 Without thinking about it too hard, look at each name and write the first word that comes into your head that you would use to describe the person. Be really honest, otherwise the exercise is pointless.

a) What is the word that describes how you see them?

3 When you have completed the exercise, look at the words you have used.

a) If you worked in a room with someone every day and they thought this way about you, what would it feel like?

b) Would you feel connection?

c) Would you feel OK?

d) Would you feel safe?

The above exercise is one of the most powerful exercises I have ever used with groups of teachers. When they look at the first thought they have and imagine meeting that every day themselves, they begin to get a glimpse of what it may be like for the child.

How thoughts and feelings affect behaviour

 We are all worms, but I do believe that I am a glow worm.
Winston Churchill

One effective exercise proves how easy it is to tell what someone thinks of you. A volunteer is asked to stand in front of the room and think about someone she really likes being around, or someone with whom she would love to spend more time. Then she is asked to let go of that one and think about someone she does not like being around. Even when she is just standing still doing nothing, it is usually very easy to read from her body language what she is thinking. When she thinks of someone she likes or wants to be around sometime very obvious differences occur: one woman kept lifting up on her toes. However, usually more subtle differences occur: the face muscles relax and even if the volunteer does not smile, she looks like she is going to; the shoulders and chest area open up as if allowing the person into the heart; the hands sometime appear more open; the eyes change very subtly and yet you can see the relaxation and pleasure in the way they seem to sparkle more and the muscles around them relax.

When the volunteer thinks of someone she does not like, the following changes may be seen: again the eyes change, often closing slightly; the muscles in the face drop and look saggy, tense or hard; the chest area closes in on itself; sometimes the arms move into a defensive position across the stomach or chest; even the hands occasionally clench.

Then the volunteer is asked to describe something she really likes doing, or something interesting she has done. While the volunteer is telling the audience, she is asked to think about one of the audience and imagine the person is there with her. Again they see the same body language and often there is a slight alteration in voice tone, speed and volume. Usually it is so obvious to the audience which member has been chosen that the reaction is one of shock. The very best way to observe these signs is to watch someone when they are not aware you are watching them; for example, I once worked in a school where the deputy head really disliked some of the staff and it was very good practice for me to watch her body changes whenever she was near them or had to speak to them.

Case study: Jimmy's story

Children are even better at picking up non-verbal messages than adults. They are not as influenced by what we say, there is something else they look for. A short while ago I was supporting a child in school who was very close to being permanently excluded. He was an Irish Traveller and found school a very difficult and unsafe place to be. We were discussing how he felt in school. He told me that everyone hated him. I asked him who exactly hated him and he replied all the teachers except three, whom he named. He claimed all the other people who worked in the school also hated him and Miss X hated him the most.

I spent some time in the school working with Jimmy and I also sat in a meeting with him and Miss X. In the meeting she said all the right things, even when I asked him to tell her how he felt and he said, 'You hate me.'

She said, 'No; I don't hate you. It's just that you break the rules and are rude. You fight with the other children and refuse to do your work. I don't hate you at all.'

So there it was. She had done her best to mention the behaviour not the child, as we are told to. Yet every non-verbal part of her was saying, 'I hate you!' or at the very least 'I intensely dislike you'. It was so obvious. When she left the room he turned to me and said, 'See. I told you she hated me.' She did, and I could not say anything to contradict that as he would have known I was lying.

Also from my time in the school and from discussions with the different staff I discovered that he was right about the three teachers who did not hate him. They found him very difficult to work with but each one of them said they liked him and had some understanding of how alien and difficult school was for him, and you could see they believed it.

Now look again at the list of words you used to describe each child in the previous exercise. Which ones would cause the child to feel accepted, liked, approved of, valued? Which ones would cause a child to feel not good enough, disliked, disapproved of, unacceptable?

If as adults we see children in ways that are accepting and loving, then they can grow and develop, and they feel safe. Put yourself in their position: imagine you had a boss, a headteacher, who had one of those negative thoughts about you. Would you be prepared to learn new and difficult skills in front of her? Would you feel comfortable making lots of mistakes while you practised your new skill? Would you feel comfortable receiving feedback from her? Would you receive the feedback well or might you dismiss it saying something like, 'well she doesn't like me any way' or 'she would say that about me she thinks I'm a …'?

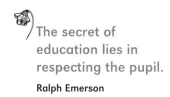

The secret of education lies in respecting the pupil.

Ralph Emerson

The other important point to consider is what can happen when we have formed hard opinions about someone that we are unwilling to review. I have a male friend who thinks I am not a very good driver. He would say, if he were asked to write down his first thoughts about me, that I am easily distracted and that I do not focus on things for long. He has not said that to me directly for years, and yet I feel it every time I get in the car with him. Normally I am an excellent driver, but guess what happens when I am driving him: I lose concentration, I miss turnings, I do things I never usually do, even though I am trying really hard to prove him wrong and show him I am a good driver. When we know that a person has formed a consistent view about us, it has an effect on how we behave when we are in their presence.

This is why some children behave very differently when they are in the company of certain adults. If your thought about them is that they are annoying, then they will be. If your thought about them is that they are cheeky, slow, kind, helpful, clever, then it will be very difficult for them not to be that way around you.

If you do not believe this to be true, start watching yourself and notice how different you are around various people, then write down what you think each of them thinks about you. You will begin to see why you are the way you are in their presence.

How do we connect?

 Do not free a camel of his hump; you may be freeing him from being a camel.

G.K. Chesterton

To connect with each child in our care, we need to think that they are OK, that there is nothing wrong with them, that they are beautiful, wonderful children at the early stages of their life. They want so much to be loved, to be accepted, to belong and to feel OK. Why can we not just see that, just see these beautiful little children? Answer: because our perception of each child changes according to our wants, our needs, our judgements and our emotions. We forget what it was like not to know, not to be skilled at these things, and we forget that we are not so different, that we have not moved so far ourselves.

Children's behaviour may annoy you, frustrate you, or delight you. However, we need to remember that is only their *behaviour* that annoys us, not the children themselves. They are, like all of us, a work in progress; they get it right and they get it wrong. They are trapped by fear, anger and disappointment, just as we are, and their amygdala traps them, just as ours does.

If you are willing, go down your list and highlight all the children with whom you feel you have not connected. In particular, highlight all those with a comment next to their name that you would not like people to think about you. Now over the next weeks, get to know and like each one of those children – if necessary, start with just one child. Look for the good and think a different thought about the child – even if you do not really believe it at first, just imagine it is true. Think, 'You are wonderful' and imagine it is true, no matter what the child does.

Act it out, but do it as a real actor. Your performance must be believable, because children are such emotional barometers that they will detect insincerity almost immediately. What you will find is that, after a short while, you will begin to believe it. Then the child will believe it and begin to feel wonderful; indeed, it is amazing how different that child will be after a short while. Children respond really quickly once they feel accepted, truly accepted, and loved (see Chapter 8 for an explanation of Psychological Laws).

If you have never experienced being around someone who thinks you are really wonderful, then you will find it hard to imagine how it feels. If you *have* had that experience with a parent, teacher, aunt, partner – anyone – then you know how it feels. You can try anything because the unconditional love is so freeing; you can risk failing or be courageous because you feel safe and loved. They think you are wonderful no matter what you do; it is not what you do that makes them love you, it is just you.

Surely we want children to be this free in school, free enough to reach their absolute potential.

The Prophecy

There was once a small monastery, a community rather down at heel that was thinking of disbanding. Then one night the abbot had a vision in prayer. The revelation was simple and short – 'One of your number is the Messiah.'

He shared his vision with the rest of the community. And from that day onwards, things started to change because when each was with another member of the community he would think, 'Perhaps this one is the one.' So they began to treat one another with great love and care and respect.

When they got up in the morning and looked in the mirror they thought, 'Perhaps I am the One' so they began to treat themselves with great love and care and respect. And so the community began to grow. People from far and wide came to join and soon the community that had been dying came to thrive, grow and prosper.

Values and Visions[1]

Intrinsic and extrinsic motivation: its effects on behaviour and learning

 Perhaps the most important single cause of a person's success or failure educationally has to do with the question of what he believes about himself.
A.W. Combs

Many schools at present operate behaviour management/modification systems based on rewards: children get stickers, gold stars, certificates and special time. These are used to induce/seduce children into behaving in the way the school wants. Children who are able to sit still and be quiet get rewarded; children who finish work or help someone get rewarded. There are numerous great reasons for celebrating success, or celebrating achievement, no matter how big or small.

However, in many schools the achievement that is recognised often has nothing to do with developing the internal values of the child. The school is simply using the motivation of approval to achieve more socially acceptable behaviour. However, the difference between this and a more consciously developed intrinsic motivation is the difference between those people who perform anti-social actions away from home, or in a peer group (as with football hooligans), and those who would not smash up places and people no matter who was or was not looking as they have too much respect for property and individuals.

There are various reasons why constantly giving out stickers and certificates as the main core of a behaviour policy is not always good practice. At best it can be a wasted opportunity to develop children's intrinsic motivation; at worst it can develop and ingrain dangerous patterns of behaviour that could lead to a generation of people whose only motivation is to please or be part of any group in which they find themselves.

Wasted opportunities

Case study: Mark's story

Recently I worked with a child who was considered to have emotional and behavioural difficulties, plus learning difficulties. Mark had developed very good strategies for avoiding work that he felt he could not do, or in which he was not interested. I was asked to work with him on his emotional and behavioural difficulties and, during our initial conversation, he told me about his longing to be able to read 'proper paperback books' like the other boys in the class. I asked him to choose a book he would really like to be able to read, and he picked *The BFG* by Roald Dahl. He was not even close to this level of reading, so I asked him if he would like me to work out a plan of action that would take him towards being able to read it to himself.

He asked if he would be able to read it by the next week, and I replied that I was not sure how long it would take. If I had given him a realistic time plan, he would have given up. So we drew up an action plan that involved someone reading *The BFG* to him. Then, working on sections of it, he made his own BFG book that he built up as the reader progressed. He tried to use some of the words from the original text, because they were words he liked. He did work during literacy hour on the text of *The BFG* and gradually began to recognise large sections of the book. If he could read one or two sentences, he could remember where they came from in the story and was able to read the rest of the section getting fairly close to the correct words.

Mark's emotional and behavioural difficulties seemed to vanish during this time and he was allowed to work on the project during different lessons, lessons that he usually disrupted. In the beginning, his teacher had problems with my methods and felt Mark should be made to do the same work as everyone else. However, in time, she began to see such a difference in him that she started encouraging and supporting him. She allowed him to share his successes with the rest of the class and, in turn, the whole class began to support him.

Mark felt satisfied when he was able to pick up *The BFG* on his own in his bedroom and read it. It may not have been word perfect, but who does not skip or substitute words when reading something challenging?

You are a child and the thing you would like more than anything is to be able to read a particular book. Imagine no one knows: no one ever knows how much you long to be able to read this book, on your own, to yourself. You are given stickers for this and that. You can sit still and listen to boring stories you are not even interested in, or do simple work sheets that are meant to help you, and you will get a star. Sometimes you are set a target – you have to stop shouting out – and every lesson you get a sticker if you manage it. Sometimes you remember, sometimes you do not. None of this, however, has anything to do with that book you want to read, and as the terms go by and the teachers change, you still cannot read that book. All the stickers seem so pointless, and you feel angry and hopeless.

Case study: Mary's story

In some schools the whole concept of praise and reward is taken to a new level. It is linked with *aspirations* and *values* and introduces intrinsic motivation.

Some time ago I was working with an Irish Traveller girl called Mary. She had reached the stage in her school life where many of her peers had begun to drop out of education, or get excluded. She was 10 years old and, up until Year 5, had been a friendly, outspoken girl who was liked by the staff. She found reading and writing difficult but was able to do both. She had begun to find the work expected of her in school very demanding but was much too proud to admit it, so she had started to look for ways to avoid the work.

Her behaviour began to change dramatically and within a month she had blacked two children's eyes, destroyed a child's clay model, refused to take part in an assembly and often had a tantrum during literacy and other lessons. She was on report, which meant she was being monitored every lesson and every break. She was supposed to get a minimum of five smiley faces per day and was failing, miserably. So I was asked to speak to her.

I did have a relationship with this child – to be able to carry out work of this kind it is essential for a relationship to be built. Would you discuss your real aspirations with just anyone, least of all someone you did not think even liked you? Would you discuss your behaviour and whether it is really working or just feeding your temporary goals with someone you did not trust?

I set out to help this child see whether the behaviour she was displaying was getting her closer or further from her aspirations. Sometimes our behaviour is meeting our short-term goals, but not our long-term ones.

We discussed what had been happening using the ABC method (see page 49) and I pointed out the changes in her behaviour, mainly because she was saying she did not understand what all the fuss was about. She began to see that her behaviour was having an effect and she recognised the effect it was having.

Then I asked her about her future and what she saw herself doing. She said she did not want to get married at sixteen as most of her cousins had. She would like to get a job and to change the way people saw Travellers. She went on to talk about her temper and how the children with the black eyes had asked for it. She explained that it was the Travellers' way – if someone gets mouthy with you, you hit them, hard. She felt that she had let these children get away with it for too long, well, no more.

I asked her if that was the way of all Travellers, or was there anyone in her family who was different. She said her grandfather was very different. She told me the story of her grandmother and grandfather going into a pub where the landlord refused to serve Travellers. Her grandfather had left the pub and gone to the

Race Relations people. They had put a wire on him and sent him back to the pub. He had also gone to many other pubs and the publicans had been taken to court. Her grandfather had appeared on television and was very highly thought of in the Traveller community.

I asked her what the rest of her family would have done in the same situation. She replied that they would have smashed up the pub. They would have seen it as the Travellers' way – you do not let people treat you like that. I asked her what they would have achieved long term from smashing up the pub, and she looked me straight in the eye and said, 'Well, it just makes them right about us doesn't it? They say they won't let us into pubs because we cause fights.'

I enquired whether that behaviour earned the Traveller community what they wanted, which was respect and equality, and she replied no. Yet she could see that her grandfather's way could begin to gain them respect.

Our consequent conversations were all about her choices and whether she chose to follow her grandfather's leads, work at school, manage her temper and be someone who was a spokesperson for her people. She saw for herself in one of these conversations that she became scared and angry when she could not do the work in class and that she then reacted in the pattern she had built up since childhood.

She made a great effort to change the pattern and work on her amygdala reaction. But she only did this because it had now become important to her. It was part of her aspirations and linked to something she valued. Any amount of punishment or positive behaviour management would not have affected this child.

A target book was now introduced for Mary, at her request, so that she could record how often she wanted to smash someone and how often she managed to control it. The teacher would never have realised how frequently Mary was successful if Mary had not been able to do this. The teacher had no idea how often the other children provoked Mary. What she would have seen were Mary's failures. To an uninformed observer, Mary might have been perceived to fail each break, yet ten times every break she was actually succeeding. Would we do as well as Mary if the children were provoking us as much?

Dangerous patterns

If children are constantly motivated using extrinsic motivation, whether the motivation is moving them away from something (*fear*) or moving them towards it (*acceptance*), patterns of emotional response are built up. These are the patterns we develop to please people and get *accepted* and the patterns we develop in response to *fear* – the fight, flight, freeze and flock reactions – which the amygdala is very efficient at developing.

 Habit is habit, and not to be thrown out of the window by any man, but coaxed downstairs one step at a time.

Mark Twain

To understand how and why continual use of extrinsic motivation is dangerous, we need to look at the developmental stages of children.

In the very early phases of child development is the egocentric stage – all the baby knows is what it wants. This stage is all about 'I want' – 'if I want it, I should have it' and as it is in the very early phase, the infant has no understanding of anyone else's needs. There is no point in our getting annoyed with the baby, it does not know any different yet.

If the baby is parented well and the tantrums and demands are just accepted but not given into, normally it moves into the 'I must belong and get approved of' stage. Here it wants to be part of the community and acts in ways that it hopes will get it liked. Everything is very 'black or white' – 'If I see smiles, that means I'm liked and loved; if I see cross faces, that means I am not loved.' Children will often say to their parents 'you don't love me any more' just because the parent is cross. It is also the stage where we develop the good versus bad syndrome – a child is either good or bad.

Next the child will move into 'I'll be nice to you, if you'll be nice to me', and fairness is very important to them. They do not see why they have to be in control if you are not. They will challenge the 'do as I say not as I do' behaviours of adults, 'you shout don't you', 'I've seen you do that'. 'It's not fair' is said fairly frequently at this time. Adults often use this stage of development to bargain with children as a means of motivation, 'You do this for me and I'll do that for you.'

Then we move on to the stage where children/adults begin to understand about doing things for the community, playing in the school team for the good of the school and not just personal reward. This stage is where they become aware of the importance of the community and realise that sometimes our own personal needs or wants must be put aside for the benefit of the community. 'This is not what is expected at this school' is motivating at this level.

Lastly, there is the stage where we realise that every individual is valuable and important, and that every individual on the planet deserves our respect – not because of what they do but because they are an individual person. At this stage the rights of the individual are the most important and not the wants of the individual, as in the first stage. Here we motivate by using empathy and compassion. We say things like 'how do you feel?' and over time we gradually allow children to develop a sense of value of other people. The only real way to support children to develop this level of motivation is to model it. They need to be at the receiving end of it to begin to understand it.

If we look at the way we support children's development in schools, we can see which stages we are appealing to and which ones we are often keeping children at. Also, if we look at our own behaviour, we can see stored patterns of behaviour that we still use that come from different stages of our development. This is why we often find ourselves behaving in ways that do not match the beliefs and values we hold now.

There are some children in schools who remain at the first level of development. They are very egocentric and have very little understanding of other people's needs. If we tell them 'no', 'bad' or 'wrong', they will usually just have a tantrum.

If children are at the second stage and we say those words, they think we mean *them*; they think *they* are bad, *they* are wrong. They also interpret it as 'she doesn't like me' and consequently do not feel as though they belong. Here is where the content in Chapter 7 is essential; children in this stage of development *need* to understand by the way adults connect with them that it is safe, they do belong and they are approved of.

If we as adults reward a child for a behaviour or action that we want, then we should be aware we are probably establishing a pattern within that child. She needs to seek our approval, know she belongs and know that she can achieve this by meeting our expectations. If we punish a child for not doing what we want, again patterns build up – 'That look means she doesn't like me.' It does not matter that it is not true, during this particular stage of development it *feels* true. This pattern is now established and how many of us still have it? I know I have. Someone we know loves us looks at us a certain way and immediately we feel unloved – that look = doesn't love me – and we all have our pattern of responses to that feeling. Children at this stage of development are motivated by our approval: the adult smiles, makes approving statements and the child feels OK. We must be very careful not to abuse that. If we use our cross face and smiley face on children at this stage of development, we must be sure about the message it is giving. What do you mean when you look crossly at a young child?

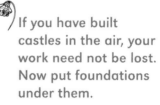

If you have built castles in the air, your work need not be lost. Now put foundations under them.

Osa Johnson

The fear of not being approved of also sets up patterns. Some children do not feel as if they belong and do not feel approved of, they see all sorts of conformation for these beliefs in the looks and words of those around them. They are in a state of fear a lot of the time. This pattern will often stay with people all their lives; if during this crucial stage of development they do not feel as if they fit in and belong, then the looks, sounds and feelings are stored and a pattern of responses will be automatically repeated. If the amygdala gets a hint of not being approved of, it will automatically revert to its fight, flight, flock and freeze patterns. We know that all children want approval at this stage of their development and so we use this knowledge to get them to do what we want. However, we may be leaving them with a lifelong set of patterns they will then need to break.

However appealing the concept of a classroom full of compliant children might be, the fact remains that children at a particular stage could be behaving in the ways that we want purely to get approval, or could be behaving in negative ways through fear of disapproval. Their motivation is intrinsic and extrinsic. The intrinsic part at this stage is the internal need to be liked and approved of. The rewards stickers and other items could give them this feeling, however, connecting with the adults around them, feeling accepted and approved of is more easily done in other ways. As they begin to feel as if they do indeed belong, they will move to the next stage and so on. Our job is to support them to develop into the final stage and to be motivated by respect for the individual. Then they will be seeking to behave in ways where they respect everyone. However, most adults are not even consistently at that stage. They are often still at the 'I'll be nice to you, if you are nice to me' stage: they will be respectful of children and adults who are respectful of them, but are not ready to model the level of respect where 'I will respect you no matter what you do'.

One other very dangerous result of children's remaining in the stage of needing approval is that, eventually, adult approval will become less important to children. The danger of this sort of pattern being built up over a period of years is that it will become very difficult to shake off. Young people become teenagers and, sometimes, the only approval they then seek is from their peers.

What we achieve inwardly will change outer reality.

Otto Rank

What happens then when their peers take drugs, or 'bunk off' school, or simply have the latest designer gear? The young person has been programmed to fit in, to behave in ways that get approval. They have no other pattern and no other way of looking at the situation. They will have to do as the group does. Not being approved of is the worst feeling and this has been confirmed over and over by us.

How do we change patterns and how do we introduce conscious intrinsic motivation?

One way is to encourage children to ask themselves what they want: What sort of picture do they want to be able to draw right now? What sort of story would they be happy with? Which book would they like to be able to read? What sort of person do they want to be? First, they need to feel safe and approved of for just being them. They need to know they will always be approved of no matter what they do, since what they do is just behaviour and usually a response to something. They need to know that we have also not sorted out all our behaviours yet. If the *only* reason for doing a piece of work is to get a star or a sticker or to please the teacher, the motivation is extrinsic and feeding into the intrinsic need for approval. If the star is a celebration of work the child is proud of, then the motivation is intrinsic in a different way, it is satisfaction in what they have achieved. Children need to be proud of their work; the child has to be doing it for a reason that means something to them, something they perceive to be of value.

If I want to be a cab driver one day, I could be motivated to develop a good memory, learn to read maps, have good interpersonal skills, understand how an engine works, develop good mental maths and a multitude of other things. If I would really like to have lots of friends, I could be motivated to develop all sorts of interpersonal and intrapersonal skills and understandings.

The star chart story

A teacher once asked me if I disapproved of star charts. When I asked her if she used one, she said she did. She was very defensive about it and told me how well it worked. I asked her how it worked, how the children gained stars, how was this decided, who was able to allocate stars to the children, and whether her own name was on the star chart.

It transpired that the children got stars for all sorts of things. The teacher decided what, and only the teacher or other teachers taking her class could allocate stars. And no, she was not on the chart. I asked for specific examples of why stars were allocated and when she decided to give them. Sometimes she gave them for the first to finish, sometimes for good work and sometimes for good behaviour. When asked why 'sometimes', the reply was long, but the short version was basically that it depended on how she felt, what she wanted and what her focus was.

I asked if she perceived the star chart as a motivator and in what way did it motivate. She said the children all wanted to get stars and they liked to see who had the most. I asked how the children knew how to get them. The reply was that the children watched for the sorts of behaviours that merited stars. These behaviours included such things as being the first person to sit up straight and listen, or being kind to someone, or producing good work. I asked if the children knew which things she was focusing on at which times and she said 'they only have to watch and see.'

To change a star chart to a consciously intrinsic motivator that was not about getting approval, the children would have to pick something they want to develop or improve over a day, a week, or a lesson. Then they give themselves a star if they think they are successful, or a partner gives them one, or the teacher does, or all three can give stars. Whoever gives the star has to be able to say specifically why they have given it. It is very important that the feedback is specific. Now the children have something to work towards; they feel different when a star is placed on the chart, they are clear why they have received it and it matters to them in a different way to 'Good, Miss is pleased with me'. It is not the star that matters or the amount, but what it represents.

> Live according to your highest light and more light will be given.
>
> **Peace Pilgrim**

One school I work in on a regular basis has the children's targets, which are designed jointly between themselves and their teachers, stuck on the table in front of where they sit. At certain points in every lesson the teacher asks them, 'Is there an opportunity for you to work on one of your targets right now?' or 'How are you doing with your targets at the moment?' In some classes they reward themselves and each other when they feel they have taken a step closer to the target.

Using aspiration posters to develop conscious intrinsic motivation

If we are to support children or adults to be more consciously intrinsically motivated, first we have to allow them to practise looking at what is important to them, as I have stated above. Next they need to begin creating the vision of how it will look, sound and feel when they have created their inner values as an external reality. One way of doing this is the creation of aspiration posters or models. Children can create posters about themselves and how they want to be by the end of term, or the end of the week. They can also use them in conjunction with targets, by making a poster that depicts them when the targets are reached.

Children like to create their aspiration posters in a variety of ways, which may not necessarily be in the form of a poster. Some children may want to create a song, a poem or a play, others may like to create a 3D model, or a collage. There are many ways in which children or adults can think about and represent their aspirations. Children need to be encouraged to be multi-sensory when developing their aspirations. The first questions they need to address are: What will success look like? What will it sound like? How will it feel? They can then begin to develop a representation of this aspiration.

The surprise motivation story

Staff at a tutorial centre for young people excluded from school were working on intrinsic motivation and how to motivate these young people to want to learn. They asked the young people to produce their own aspiration posters. Several of the posters displayed pictures of very expensive cars and other material items. The staff were disappointed that the young people had only chosen material things and were convinced that these were extrinsic motivations. So the next step for the staff was to work with the young people on why they wanted these things. They needed to look at the intrinsic motivation behind the choices.

The staff asked the young people what they thought a flash car would give them and how it would make them feel. One of the common answers was 'successful'. These were young people who had been excluded and did not feel at all successful. They were then asked what being successful would feel like. They decided they would feel happy, respected and valued. Next they were asked if the car would make them feel successful in the future. Was there anything they could easily do that would make them feel a little of that success immediately? Was there something they could do that would make them feel successful every day?

This is the beginning of conscious intrinsic motivation. Until the young people did the exercise they did not realise the motivation behind the desire for a car. If they wait for the car to give them the feeling of success they so value, it is very unlikely they will ever have such a car, unless they steal it and then would it really give them such a feeling of success. It was also interesting that behind the need for success was the need to be valued, respected and happy. Now we know that the person they aspire to be is a happy, respected and valued person, we can support them to begin to look for a way they could create this.

The real measure of our wealth is our worth if we lost our money.

Anonymous

Another way is to use the aspiration poster as a motivation and a key to change is by using the poster based on the Psychological Laws. In his book *The Act of Will,* Assagioli[1] talks about various psychological functions and their relationship to one another. He classifies them as: Sensation; Emotion-Feeling; Impulse-Desire; Imagination; Thought; Intuition; and Will. He says that there are two kinds of interactions between these functions, 'First, those that take place spontaneously, one might say mechanically; second, those that can be influenced, governed, and directed by will.'

When we are consciously choosing to change a behaviour or thought pattern based on our values, we need to be directing our psychological functions by the use of our Will.

Assagioli states that using the Psychological Laws and the techniques based on them will support us to use our Will skilfully instead of forcefully. He likens it to moving a car by pushing it (using force) or, alternatively, learning how it works and driving it (using skill).

There are ten Psychological Laws and two of them can be used in relation to this process:

Law 1. Images or mental pictures and ideas tend to produce the physical conditions and the external acts that correspond with them.

Law 2. Attitudes, movements, and actions tend to evoke corresponding images and ideas; these, in turn, evoke or intensify corresponding emotions and feelings.

Roberto Assagioli

This works in the following way. We now know the young people want to feel happy, respected and valued, so we ask them to create a poster that represents them that way: How would they sound? What sorts of things would they say? How would they look? What would other people around them see when they looked at them? How would other people feel when they were around them?

When someone has created an aspiration poster, collage or model, they have hopefully been taken through the process of visualising themselves achieving their aspirations. Asking how success will feel, look and sound begins to evoke the feelings within the person. He can then recognise that feeling and every time he looks at the aspiration poster he can evoke the feelings again.

Using this process helps a person to ascertain whether his behaviour is really working in his favour. He can look at the short-term (often negative) goals that drive his behaviour and the long-term goals to which he aspires. He can be invited to talk about his aspirations and who he aspires to be. He can then be asked what he (the person in the poster) would do in this situation. How would he (the person in the poster) feel if this happened? Because he has created a very full mental, emotional and physical image of himself, the external acts that go with that image are easy to foresee. He can already visualise doing them and feeling them. He is being encouraged to be that person now as the different image will create different thought patterns and emotions, and different emotions will create different behaviours. It is simple; he just pretends to be that person and so acts like that person.

> All great discoveries are made by those whose feelings run ahead of their thinking.
>
> C.H. Parkhurst

In 1986, researcher Robert Hartley[2] demonstrated that children are able to significantly improve their performance when they attempt tasks in the role of the cleverest pupil in the class. However, in this research the children go on to disown their success as someone else's work, 'Somebody else was doing them. I bet when I do them I get them all wrong.' We are pretending to be that which we already are – the children are clever, the children doing the aspiration posters are already that person, they just have not learned to be that person yet. When you pretend something that is the truth, it will happen – you need to keep pretending. What will also support this is if the people around you also pretend. It is like the story of the giraffe who had always thought he was an antelope. One day he met some giraffes who said, 'You are a giraffe.' He said, 'No, no I am an antelope' because he had been playing out the role of antelope all his life and he believed it. So a smart giraffe said, 'OK, pretend. Pretend to be a giraffe for a while', and when the giraffe began to pretend that which was true, he became it.

Some children think they are a failure, bad or hopeless, and they believe it, so act out their lives as if it were true. They came into this world beautiful, little, perfect beings and that is what they still are. However, they took on this role, the one that seemed to fit what they were experiencing, and so they came to believe the role and thought that was who they were. Then they act as if that were the truth. What if we could pretend they were wonderful? What if we could see beyond the behaviour that does not work very well and the acting out of the role they think they are? What if, like the clever giraffe, we could see who they really are and get them to pretend it? I promise you they would become it if they pretended it for long enough, and they would become it much quicker if you pretend it as well.

Intrinsic motivation and values: their effects on behaviour

In choosing or becoming aware of values we adopt as the motivations for our behaviour, we assign worth or importance to an aspect of life, which, in turn, influences how we approach life ... There is universal recognition of a hierarchy of values which ascends from the lower material values to those higher spiritual values such as peace, love, care, selflessness, and generosity ... The twelve higher values described – co-operation, freedom, happiness, honesty, humility, love, peace, respect, responsibility, simplicity, tolerance, and unity – are core values fundamental to the well being of humanity as a whole. They will touch the core of an individual, perhaps inspiring positive change ... the world will automatically become a better place when each individual becomes a better person.

Brahma Kumaris[3]

Exercise

A valuable exercise to do with adults, children or on your own is a simple look at values.

1   Distribute cards to a group of people on which the higher values quoted above are written.

2   Each person chooses five cards or can be asked to write down five values of their own.

    The most common choices are Family, Health, Friends, Home and Happiness. If you are doing this on you own, look at the higher values but then write down the five things you value the most. By things I do not necessarily mean material things.

3   Now they are told that something has happened that means they have to give up one of their values.

    The first one is usually a big struggle. Do the same if you are on your own, give up one thing you value.

4   Once the card has been discarded, they share in pairs what it was like and how life would feel if they lost this value. If you are on your own, write this down as it will probably have more impact that way.

5   Next they have to lose another because, as before, something has happened.

    Again, choosing can be difficult and sometime they refuse. If this happens, say you will just take one at random. This always works and they always choose.

6   You can go on until there is only one value left to see what you value most at this present time.

The discussion that arises from this exercise is always amazing; it varies with different groups but is a wonderful exercise to do. People really allow themselves to feel and imagine what life would be like without one of their key values. Doing this work with young people is richly rewarding as you can begin to see them really take on these values. One of the questions that can be asked is, 'What might happen in real life that could cause this value to be taken away?' Some young people who had been permanently excluded from school stated that this had taken away their feeling of self-respect, which they valued a lot.

A group of young people doing drugs prevention work were asked if using some of these drugs, including alcohol, could cause them to lose some of the things they valued. The discussion was very, very different from the one about why using drugs is dangerous. The motivation was consciously intrinsic and values based. Were their friends more valuable than their families? Was their health more valuable than anything? Which of the choices would truly bring them happiness? They even talked about people they knew who stole money for drugs and discussed the loss of freedom, family and friends.

The exercise overleaf, which is an extension of the values exercise, was used in a workshop for parents. Some parents were shaking their heads and were asked if they were willing to share with the group what they had noticed. One mother was very tearful and said that one of her five values was joy. She explained that her life was so stressed she had no time for joy and if her family were asked if she valued joy, they would deny it. She revealed that she had no desire to go on living in this way. She was asked if she wanted to change the value, but she refused. She really did value joy but she wanted to know what to do. The suggestion was to do something each day, something small, that would bring her joy. If you consciously behave as if you value something, it starts to become a reality.

Children model much of their behaviour from significant people around them. My granddaughter copies a great deal of what I do and takes on many of my values. For example, I value all living things and will not kill deliberately, not even an ant. At age three she had already begun to copy this. One day I hope she will be supported to look at those values and what they really mean to her, and also be encouraged to take on what is appropriate for her and what she believes. As one of the values she has taken on at the moment is respect for life, she therefore finds it very distressing when she sees people killing wasps or spiders. In her nursery she made a big fuss when one of the teachers killed a wasp and told her she was very naughty. Her behaviour was seen as disruptive as her values were not in line with those of the teacher.

Children come to school with different values and our first job is to respect their right to have values, even if they are the opposite to ours, and to give them an opportunity to examine them. Even young children will say that they value respect and that everyone deserves respect. In circle time I have always worked on values as a way of checking if our behaviour is in line with our values. As a teacher, I have to be prepared to ask the children if they feel I am treating them all with respect and be ready to hear if anyone feels I do not respect them. If I model this sort of behaviour, then I can encourage the children to do the same.

Exercise

Try this exercise.

1 Write a list of the ten things (I do not mean only material things) you value the most.

2 Now look at the list and answer this question honestly: Do you behave and make choices that truly reflect these values?

   a) If you have health on your list, what do you do to keep yourself healthy?

   b) If you have family, do you visit them often? Do you argue or upset them more than you would like?

3 Check for yourself if your behaviour is in line with your values. If you were filmed for a few weeks, could the audience tell from how you live your life what is important to you?

4 Now cross out all the things you do not really act as though you value, and be honest with yourself. Only put them back on if and when you are prepared to act as though they are of value.

If we want children to behave in line with the highest values, then we have to model that behaviour ourselves and children need to know why we are doing it. Sometimes teachers believe that if we do not punish a child, then the other children will think we are letting them get away with things. Children know when we have great respect for all of them and would not expect us to treat a child badly, even if they had done the most awful things. They can also know when we respect ourselves. If you want to check if your school is a model of higher values, ask yourselves these questions:

Human beings

❀ Do we treat all people as though they matter?

❀ Are we treating human beings as unique individuals of infinite worth, each with a purpose and each with the potential to make a creative contribution?

❀ Do we regard life as sacred?

Values and visions

❀ Are we acknowledging our individual, differing and joint values and visions?

❀ Are we aware of that which gives meaning and purpose to our life, our school, and our world? Are we working from the vision we have for our school and world?

❀ Do we use our values and visions to work creatively and effectively?

Here and now

❀ Are we starting with the here and now everyday problems, opportunities and challenges that face staff and children?

❀ Do we see the present problem, be it playground aggression, gender conflict, another curriculum requirement and so on as the starting point for transformation? Are we offering support and strategies or judgements to the here and now?

                                                    Becoming Emotionally Intelligent – Catherine Corrie

Spiritual development

* ❀ Is spiritual development part of everyday life?
* ❀ Is it about how we live our lives? Are we acknowledging that there is more to life than meets the eye: are we open to the transcendent?
* ❀ Are we recognising our connectedness with all life?
* ❀ Do we make space for wonder and awe at the world around us?
* ❀ Do compassion, forgiveness and trust enter into our relationships with others?
* ❀ Is there joy and creativity in our everyday lives at school?
* ❀ Do our actions lead to justice, peace and care for the Earth?

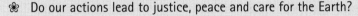

Tree of Life

Global awareness

* ❀ Are we seeing ourselves as part of a global community?
* ❀ Are we acknowledging the oneness of humanity and all life?
* ❀ Are we looking at the challenges that face the planet?
* ❀ Are we teaching about issues to do with justice, peace and care for the Earth?
* ❀ Are we enabling people to respond to the unfairness and wastefulness that we find in our daily lives?
* ❀ Are we showing within our own lives in school, ways of tackling injustice, violence and environmental abuse?

Community

* ❀ Are we creating within school a microcosm of a caring community which senses the interdependence of all people and the created universe?
* ❀ Are all individuals and groups within the community valued, involved and part of the whole?
* ❀ Are we finding shared values and visions while being sensitive to individual perspectives?
* ❀ Does our school actively demonstrate its interdependence with the local and global communities of which it is a part?
* ❀ Is our community open and inclusive – a door to the wider world?

Faith traditions

❀ Are we drawing on the insights and wisdoms of faiths?

❀ Does our work relate to those of all faiths and no faiths?

❀ Do we encourage respect for the many different faith positions?

Southern voices

❀ Are we listening to the majority of the world's people, often referred to as the Third World?

❀ Are we recognising that in many important aspects of human experience we have much to learn from other traditions, especially the South and those within our midst who are marginalised?

❀ While being aware of our similarities do we yet acknowledge when there are differences in terms of resources, power and perceptions?

Diversity

❀ Are we recognising and valuing our differences as individuals and groups?

❀ Is there dialogue over differences?

❀ Are we honouring our interdependence and one humanity?

❀ Are we working towards racial and gender equality and challenging all forms of prejudice that divide us?

Holistic approach

❀ Are we teaching in ways that encourage the development of the whole person and the whole curriculum?

❀ Are we recognising the wholeness of the individual?

❀ Are we using play, imagination, reflection and contemplation alongside reason and analysis?

❀ Are we nurturing the whole person – the physical, emotional, mental, aesthetic and spiritual? Are we looking at the school as a whole?

Creativity

❀ Are we using all our abilities and drawing fully on our natural creative resources?

❀ Are energy and aliveness present in our school?

Transformation

❀ Are we creating a school where transformation takes place; where the old is seen with new eyes?

Adapted from Sally Burns and Georgeanne Lamont[4]

If we are not considering the above, then what are we doing with the children in our care? Many people are shocked and saddened every time there is a new outbreak of violence in the Middle East, or Northern Ireland or any of the 'hot spots' on the planet. Yet we as teachers and carers of the young have a unique opportunity to move forward the evolution of human nature.

When a whole generation of children emerge with these values, able to communicate clearly and authentically, resolve conflict with care and respect and live their lives true to the above, in other words, living and acting as if life really is more important than property or land, then the wars will stop and the world will change.

As Gandhi said, 'Societal change begins within each one of us.' We have to start somewhere, and if we could do these things within our families, schools and communities, it would spread throughout the planet. Yet at the moment we fight, shout and disrespect each other, with regularity, and wonder why people are still killing each other all over the world.

The school is the microcosm of the world. What we create in school can provide a glimpse of how our world may be.

Values and Visions

Mohandas (Mahatma) Gandhi

Values and beliefs

Being proud of your beliefs and values	Prizing your beliefs and values
	Being prepared to publicly state them where appropriate
Having chosen your own beliefs and values for yourself	Having chosen them from alternatives
	Having chosen them after consideration of all the consequences
	Having chosen them freely
Making use of your beliefs and values consistently to make choices and be intrinsically motivated	Acting on your own beliefs and values even when under pressure
	Acting with consistency

Values clarification model

The above figure shows a framework for working with beliefs and values in the classroom. Children can practise sorting out their own beliefs and values, using exercises that take place within a safe and supportive environment. When they later need to make decisions about drug taking, sex, and other behaviours that will affect their futures, they will be more able to sort out what is really important to them, and not be so easily pressured into doing things that they may afterwards regret.

Within the British education system, children are expected to receive moral and spiritual education as well as academic. Traditionally, adults have tried to lead children in this by moralising to instil the values of the adult into the child, or acting as good models so that the child will pick up the 'correct' values, and sometimes assisting the child in understanding and clarifying their own values system in relation to that of the society in which they belong.

Moralising is not usually effective for several reasons. The values held by the adult may be very different from those of the child. Many teachers have very different value systems to those of the families attending the school. Also if adults moralise and their behaviour is not consistent with what they say, then children are given the message 'Do as I say not as I do.'

Some parents and schools avoid the whole issue of values and beliefs, and do not give children any frameworks to help them come to an understanding of their own values. Whether or not we are trying to influence children's values, we will. Just by being around them and interacting with them we will be demonstrating our values by our actions.

Relying on modelling as the only way of supporting children is very hit and miss. Children will be exposed to many models and having to manage them without support is not easy for children or young people. Using the values clarification model shown in the figure overleaf will enable children to explore the various beliefs and values that they hold. Practising the exercises in a safe and supported environment will enable children to experience the valuing process so that they can use it again when they have to make important life changing decisions.

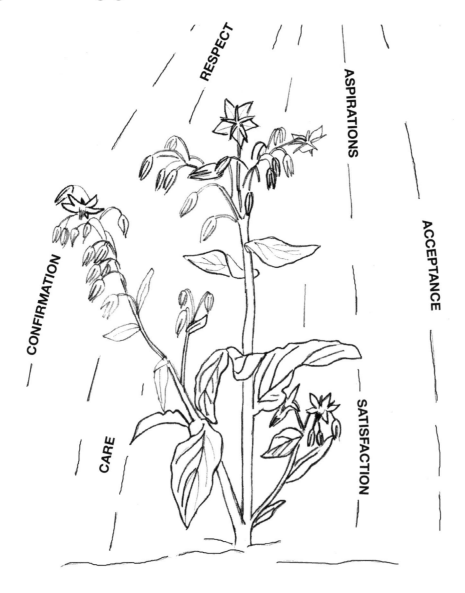

Chapter 9

Self-esteem

There are a variety of terms for what could be called our sense of self. How do we esteem ourselves? What do we feel about our own worth? How much do we respect ourselves?

All of these are interrelated: they are all affected by others and they all affect how we perceive and treat others.

> The idea expressed in the Biblical 'love thy neighbour as thyself' implies the respect for one's own integrity and uniqueness, love for and understanding of one's own self, which cannot be separated from respect and love and understanding for another individual. The love for my own self is inseparably connected with love for any other being.
>
> Erich Fromm[1]

If you could give the children in your care, or in your school, one gift, one quality, by the time they left school, which would you give them? I have asked this question of teachers, parents, governors, lunchtime supervisors and school support staff. I ask them to write down the answer and then stick it on a flip chart.

Every time the result is the same:

Self-esteem	Various others for example:
Self-worth	Love of learning
Self-respect	Love of literature
Self-love	Love of music
Self-confidence	Reaching their full potential
98%	**2%**

The next question to be asked of schools or teachers is, 'If a visitor to your school were to watch for a few weeks, would he see that this is the quality you care about most?' Sadly, most teachers shake their heads and some even cry. If parents were asked the same question, again most shake their heads and some cry.

Have parents told the schools how important this is to them? Are the teachers aware that high grades are not the very top of the list? Often parents have to admit that they have probably given schools the opposite impression. Teachers are usually shocked to find that parents and governors want the same for the children as they do. What is interesting is how low many people's self-esteem can be.

Exercises in developing self-esteem are often very good at showing you how little self-esteem the people around you really have.

Exercise

Exercise for individuals.

1   Sit in a chair and put an empty chair opposite you.

2   Close your eyes and think of someone you really love a great deal and imagine them sitting in the chair opposite you.

3   Look across at them and see them sitting there. Listen and hear their voice. How do you feel towards them?

4   Now move across to the other chair and pretend you are them and you are looking across at you. What do you see when you look at you? What do you hear? How do you feel when you see you?

   Remember to keep pretending you are the other person and you are looking at you through their eyes.

5   What words would you use to describe the you that you see and how you feel?

Exercise

Exercise for whole staff groups using a carousel.
The carousel consists of one circle within another, the inner circle having chairs facing out and the outer circle having chairs facing in. This creates pairs facing each other.

1   The person on the inside tells the person on the outside one quality or gift she has noticed the listener display in school. The listener can say nothing except thank you.

2   Then the outer circle moves around one and the exercise is repeated. This goes on; the outer circle keeps moving around until a request to stop is received, whereupon the circles swap over and the outside circle affirms the inside circle.

People generally find it extremely difficult to hear the kinds of affirmation expressed in the above exercise. What does that say about our sense of self-worth? What does it say about the way we as a society condition the young?

When we are small babies we are perfect: we have no awareness of anything wrong with us. How soon is it before we begin to develop fears about our value or worth? We only have to sit quietly for a while and listen to our own self-talk, particularly at the end of the day. We question what kind of person we are and what sort of teacher/parent/sibling/daughter/son/friend. We need to listen to the messages we give ourselves and ask ourselves these questions: Who is listening? Who is speaking?

Every snowflake and child is unique, each one an amazing creation. All you have to do is stop and look to see the beauty in each one.

Catherine Corrie

Each small baby is born with its own unique beauty, but how long are they allowed to just be perfect the way they are? For some it is no time at all, they are judged even before they leave the womb: for being the wrong gender, for not being physically perfect, for coming at the wrong time, for having the wrong father and many more. Then as they cry out after they are born, some are not welcomed, some feel rejection in the first moment of life.

It doesn't matter what we do until we accept ourselves. Once we accept ourselves, it doesn't matter what we do.

Charly Heavenrich

Is it any wonder that many beautiful, unique beings get lost and hidden behind many layers of negative thoughts and behaviour patterns, and we lose sight of who we really are.

Self-image

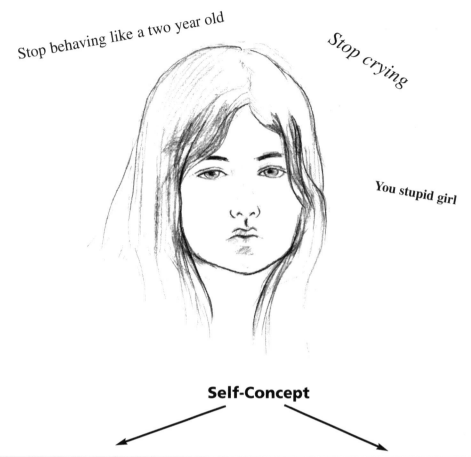

Stop behaving like a two year old

Stop crying

You stupid girl

Self-Concept

Self-Image	Ideal Self
Abilities, attributes, appearance influenced by our perception of how we are accepted and valued by significant others and our own developing values.	The person you would like to be, abilities, attributes, appearance you would like to have. Influenced by what seems to be valued by significant others.
Healthy self-image is when you accept yourself where you are now. You know your strengths, weaknesses, gifts, vulnerabilities, values and beliefs. You know they are not fixed and they can grow and develop.	Realistic ideal self is built on own values, attainable aspirations and goals and the ability to see yourself achieving them. A belief that abilities can be developed and attributes built on.

Self-Esteem

Self-esteem

When you have a healthy self-image and an accessible ideal self –
something to aspire to – then self-esteem is high. High self-esteem means
you feel a sense of
being accepted as you
are now; you feel
capable of learning,
growing and
developing, and you
and others value the
contribution you make.
You have courage,
resilience and self-
motivation.

If self-image is poor –
'I'm not good enough',
reinforced by significant
others – and ideal self is
out of reach or not in
line with your own
values and beliefs but is
what someone else
thinks you should be,
then self-esteem is low.
Low self-esteem means
difficulty trying new things, you protect what you have. You regard
disapproval as a rejection of self, not behaviour, have pessimistic thinking
styles and difficulty accepting praise.

How do young children build up their self-image? How do they know about their
attributes, abilities and appearance? Their abilities can be fed back to them through the
level of success they have, which is also linked to
expectations. Their attributes are almost always fed back
by significant others and so is their appearance.

*What we achieve
inwardly will change
outer reality.*
Otto Rank

How many of us have 'hang-ups' about our bodies
because of comments made to us as children or
adolescents? How many of us think we are 'not very'
something because of comments made to us as children or adolescents? If each of us
were to analyse our self-image closely and look at where it came from, we might be
surprised. It would be interesting to investigate how many of our doubts about our self-
worth arose from experiences at school.

Abilities

 For learners to have a true sense of their abilities they not only need to learn but also need to know that they know.
I feel therefore I am.

Richard Bandler

How we feel about our abilities is interrelated with the emotional attachments we have to the successes and failures of our lives. If we see failure as an opportunity to learn, the emotion attached to each memory of failure is a positive one.

While we can be presented with all sorts of evidence that something is true, it is not true in our model of the world until we feel that it is so. In spite of all we have learned from reason, logic or science, we do not feel that something is true until our mid-brain, the limbic system, tells us it is true.

If I feel like a failure, or I feel stupid, then what does that do for my self-image? Everything I do, or attempt to do, builds up my sense of ability. So how do we help children to feel capable and able? How do we build up their sense of understanding, knowledge and achievement?

Learners need to express negative feelings caused by upsets, fights, loss, stress or worry before being asked to learn, otherwise these feelings will adversely affect the learning. The memory stored in the hippocampus of the sensual input of the learning will be attached to the emotion present at the time of learning. Each time the learner remembers the experience, they will remember the feelings that went with it. The reptilian part of the brain always wants to avoid feelings of embarrassment, shame, humiliation, even hurt, and therefore it will not want to remember. These feelings affect the memory in a very negative way. Therefore, we need to use activities that allow pupils to generate strong, positive emotions about what they are learning. This can mean taking into account all the Accelerated Learning fundamentals to ensure learning

- ❀ is high challenge/low threat
- ❀ has high levels of sensory information
- ❀ has immediate feedback to learners
- ❀ contains activities that engage the whole brain simultaneously
- ❀ has intrinsic motivation
- ❀ is suited to the individual learning styles and intelligences.

You can deliberately create emotion-inducing experiences; for example, 'Magic Spelling'.[2] This is a visual and kinesthetic method of teaching spelling and is very effective for all learners, but particularly useful for people who already see themselves as bad spellers. If you see yourself as a bad speller, then the whole notion of spelling takes on feelings of confusion, doubt, sometimes humiliation, embarrassment, and even shame. Every time the person thinks about spelling or is unsure about a spelling, these feelings will become present, the reptilian part of the brain will try to avoid it and flight, fight, freeze or flock patterns will emerge.

Using Magic Spelling starts by teaching children how to get into a 'good' state:

1   Ask them to think of something that makes them smile, or causes them to feel 'Yes!'. They need to use a good, funny or positive memory, or even a fantasy. The important thing is the feeling it creates – they need to feel a 'good feeling'.

2   Now ask them to turn up the good feeling; I tell them to imagine a volume button in their belly and they keep pressing it, turning up the volume until often they are really laughing or at least smiling broadly.

3   Ask them to let the feeling go.

4   Ask them to get it back and turn up the volume again.

5   Keep this up until they can easily change their state.

6   You can now introduce a word you want them to learn to visualise. First, they get the good feeling and then you hold up the word, keeping the volume turned up while they look at the word. They keep looking and you keep getting them to turn up the volume.

This process allows the correct spelling to be stored in the children's visual memory and attached to the correct spelling will be a good feeling. Now when they see the word spelled correctly, they get the good feeling, and when it is not spelled correctly, there is no good feeling. Hence no more confusion.

It is important to give learners time to have positive feelings about what they learn. Never avoid emotions – deal with them. Allow learners time to de-stress before the learning takes place so that the emotions can be positively engaged to help children change their state into one that is receptive for learning. In order for the learners' sense of ability to be reinforced, they need to 'know that they know'.

In his training materials, Richard Bandler, one of the founders of Neuro-Linguistic Programming (NLP), says that our brain has three criteria that allow it to 'know what it knows'. These criteria make it possible for the limbic system to create its own self-convincers, which vary from person to person. The criteria are:

❀   reinforce the learning in your preferred modality: visual, auditory or kinesthetic.

❀   reinforce it for the right number of times: for some it is once, for others it may be three to twenty times.

❀   reinforce it for a sufficient length of time: for some it is a couple of seconds, for others it may be minutes or hours.

When we have used the above reinforcements, we believe that learning has taken place, we have a gut feeling for it, we can see it as one of our abilities and, once we believe it, it becomes part of who we are and usually says something about us.

Most of us need the above reinforcements in our preferred modality. For example, some people will say, 'I'll believe it when I see it' and, for a strongly visual learner, this visualisation is essential. For an auditory learner seeing is not believing and they might be heard saying, 'I saw it but I don't believe it.' They will have to discuss it with someone, establish whether they get agreement and then decide if they believe it or not. The kinesthetic learner will say something like, 'If I can hold it or be there and experience it, I'll believe it.'

Then there are the frequency variables, which are how much repetition we need: we will need to see it, talk about it, or experience it, ranging from three to twenty times, before we believe it.

 What lies before us and what lies behind us are small matters compared to what lies within us. And when we bring what is within out into the world, miracles happen.

Henry David Thoreau

Finally, there is the duration variable, which is the length of time that the learner needs to be looking at, discussing or doing/experiencing to affirm the information.

Changing beliefs about our abilities

The previous self-convincers are essential when it come to changing beliefs. If a learner already believes he is going to succeed, it only takes 'top-up reinforcement' to maintain that belief. If, however, a learner believes he is a failure, then you have to give him a chance to convince himself that he is a success. All three of the criteria overleaf must be met for him. If he is visual, he needs to see to believe, to see for the number of times that works for him, and to see for the length of time that works for him, otherwise his belief, or disbelief, will pertain.

There are always children on the special needs register with spelling difficulties. These children often have no other difficulty; however, their spelling begins to affect other areas that involve writing. Subsequent years will show assessments and individual education plans (IEPs) reflecting difficulties connected with a lack of development in writing skills. In some children it will also influence behaviour and they will exhibit the classic behaviours associated with people who feel they are failures.

Case study: Jason's story

Jason was in Year 5 and the paperwork in his 'special needs' file showed that the current targets were all behavioural. He was described as challenging: if he was given work to do, he often refused; he tested teachers, support staff and other pupils; he would argue his case no matter what, and always had an answer for everything. His targets were to stay on task and try to stop answering back, and to reflect on his behaviour instead of always making an excuse for it.

Two courses of action were taken. One was the ABC method. The teacher and the support assistant were asked to record the antecedents, or what happened leading up to the behaviour they did not want. They also jotted down the behaviour of the child and the behaviour of anyone who responded to him – staff or pupil – and the consequences of the behaviour. The second tactic was to look through his file and trace his progress, talking to past teachers and to his parent.

The conclusion reached was that Jason was a very visual and kinesthetic learner. He seemed to need to access both of these modalities to absorb the learning successfully. He had been taught to spell using phonics, which is auditory, and had found this very difficult. He had soon been identified as having a spelling difficulty.

As he was a very kinesthetic learner, he liked to move about, to try things out and experience first hand – watching someone else show him did not work for him. So he had soon been identified as lacking in concentration, attention seeking, unable to wait and take his turn, and demanding. He also lacked confidence in his spelling. As this school did not allow the process of creating the writing (breaking up the task into stages of creating, editing, redrafting and publication), he was expected to do the whole process in one go. This he found impossible and was thus categorised as a reluctant writer.

He started to find ways of behaving that meant he could avoid writing and that allowed him to feel some sense of power (which he lacked). He displayed the classic 'you cannot make me' and 'you cannot stop me' behaviours and so had been identified as having emotional and behavioural difficulties.

He had so little chance to write that all his writing skills fell behind: the content was not developed and remained very immature, the style was also immature, and the grammar and punctuation was non-existent due to the lack of practice.

Generally children who are seen as having 'special needs', being 'slow learners', having 'behavioural difficulties', or being 'at risk' will have inappropriate self-convincer strategies. They usually do not know what they know, will often tell you they do not know anything and have very little self-confidence. Sometimes they may self-convince too easily, which means they give up on learning very quickly, being convinced they cannot do it.

Linking this to learning, engaging the emotions at the end of the learning, can help the brain to know what it knows. As teachers we need to listen for the stamp of approval: the 'I see!', 'It feels right to me', or 'Wait till you hear this, Miss!'

Several methods of intervention were used with Jason, all designed to improve his self-esteem, self-worth, self-respect and self-confidence. The two aspects of his self-image that needed work were the feelings he had about his ability and how he felt about his attributes.

He was shown what sort of learning styles he suited the best, which he found fascinating. He discovered that he was very visual and kinesthetic and was able to see that the areas of his life where he found learning easy were those that engaged his preferred modalities; for example, sport, where he generally learned very successfully. However, even in sports he had found some difficulties. He had started martial arts classes and found them very frustrating, so he had given up very quickly. It was discovered that this was due to his lack of opportunity to practise. He had very little time during the lesson to practise and if he tried to practise in school during break, he got into trouble, and the same happened at home.

He was obviously someone who needed a lot of repetition and he needed to do it physically. Some of the children in the class could watch numerous times and learn that way, but this was not enough for Jason, even though he was very visual. Another factor was that he needed quite a long duration. He explained that when he could do the hold/move slowly, feeling how his body moved and where to balance, he began to 'feel it'. He used lots of kinesthetic language: 'You know it just feels right' and 'I need to know it feels right, otherwise I could be doing it wrong'. So he wanted to feel the correct moves, then practise them lots of times, then he felt confident to use them.

The Magic Spelling strategy was used, concentrating on the internal state and getting the 'good feeling'. This was explained fully to Jason so that he was able to take responsibility for his own learning and take credit for the success (see page 103). It was important that he did not see this as magic but knew it came from being taught in a way he was able to use, in addition to his willingness to really engage in the process. Teachers worked slowly so he could feel his way through, with kinesthetic language used to check how he was progressing. When he began to feel his way through the process, he then practised and began to have success. He could look up and see the word in class, and when he needed to write, he began to have a few successes.

He started to change his belief from 'I'm rubbish' to 'I can do this', yet there was still a note of surprise when he said it. Gradually, Jason became more willing to try things and knew what worked successfully for him. He understood that his modality variable, frequency variable and duration variable were just his way of learning, his way of feeling he knew how, his way of feeling capable. This gave Jason a sense of power. He now knows that, for his learning to be optimised, these variables need to be met and he needs to be willing to be responsible for their being met. If he does not achieve success immediately, it no longer confirms the 'I'm rubbish' statement he had taken on. He can now look at what is missing and get support with it, which is in line with 'I can do this'.

Those who emphasise 'covering the content' are outdated. Provide learners with resources to construct their own way of understanding the material. This in turn, gives the learner time to have positive feelings about it and to succeed. Increased learner self-confidence follows, along with intrinsic motivation for future learning.

Jensen[3]

There are many ways to support the learners in and out of the classroom to celebrate learning. Alistair Smith has many examples in his books *The Alps Approach*[4] and *Accelerated Learning in Practice*.[5] These activities seal the information or experience in the brain as real and worth remembering, since memories attached to strong positive emotions are usually much easier to recall. To ensure that all the children in the class leave knowing that they know, we need to provide a range of ways for validating their learning. Some will need to discuss it, teach it to a peer, role-play, write a learning poster or journal, or take part in some form of group activity such as a concept map, or brainstorm. The activities must use all three modalities, last for several minutes, and be carried out with several people or done several times.

The ideal self

During Emotional Intelligence workshops with school staff I often ask them to write down their description of the ideal teacher. Sometimes I give them this task after providing them with some quotes, such as the two on this page.

The wise teacher does not ask you to enter the house of his wisdom. He leads you to the threshold of your own mind.

Kahlil Gibran

My Ideal Mother

loving
responsible
capable
caring
organised
fun loving
happy
affectionate
patient

Teachers affect eternity; no one knows where their influence stops.

Anon

The reason I do the quotes is because it always seems to influence how the teachers respond. When I do not use them, the ideal teacher is noticeably different than when I do. As a starting point, this is significant. You could ask yourself what outside influences affect your notion of the ideal teacher, wife, mother, father, husband, partner, daughter, or son.

We all play many different roles in life and our perception of ourselves within each one is always a combination of our self-image and how we think we should be in that role, that is, our ideal self.

Many new mothers have, or know friends who have, very low self-esteem as mothers. This low self-esteem is often due to repeated comments made by their own mother, mother-in-law, partner or some other significant person. Sometimes the comments were not meant unkindly, but were about Mary or Goppi and how her baby does not seem to cry so much, or is drinking from a cup already, and so on. I recently visited a friend whose baby was two weeks old. She had just had a visit from the midwife who has been concerned about the baby's weight. The baby looked happy and contented but apparently was not gaining weight as expected. My friend was in tears, distraught, saying 'I'm a hopeless mother. There must be something wrong with my milk. My poor baby, I'm letting him down.' The comments are of lesser importance than the construction made by the listener. So a good mother would have a baby who didn't cry so much = I don't measure up as a mother. A good mother would have a baby who gained the correct weight = I am not a good enough mother. If the listener is able to shrug off the comment, then her model of the ideal mother is probably strong and personal, or the person making the comment is not significant to the listener.

Exercise

Check you own self-esteem and who it is based on.

1 Consider your own most significant role; this may be you as parent, your job, whatever.

2 Write down the characteristics, attributes, abilities and appearance of the perfect person in this role; for example, what would the perfect parent be like, in your opinion.

3 Look at your list. To what, or to whom, are you comparing yourself?

 It is usually a combination of several people. If I had Susan's organisation and time management skills, John's interpersonal skills, Brian's self-confidence and Sukvia's energy, then I would be great at my job.

4 Ask yourself how close you are to this perfect mother, teacher, carer.

 If you are a long way from it, then it is likely your self-esteem in this role is low and your fear level is high.

 If you are reasonably close to it, then it is likely your self-esteem will be high in this role and you will feel safe and secure.

 If you wish to change the level of your self-esteem in this area, you can check the list of characteristics, skills, attributes and appearance you have given the perfect one and decide if you wish to change them. Are they realistic?

There is nothing wrong with comparing our abilities and attributes to those of others – it is often how we grow and develop. We see an attribute in others to which we aspire and we model it. We do not want to be them, or even do it exactly like them, but there are aspects of what they do that we perceive as useful, so we watch, ask questions, try things out, ask for feedback – and thus we develop.

So when is this modelling healthy and when does it become a tool by which to damage our self-esteem? A mother is told, 'Mary's baby doesn't cry so much, and sleeps through the night.' If a mother is concerned about her baby crying and has any feelings of insecurity, then using the Neurological Levels model taken from Neuro-Linguistic Programming (shown below) can help explain her situation.

Neurological Levels Model

Spirituality	What is the highest thought you could have about yourself? What difference do you want to make in your family/community?
Identity	What kind of identity statements do you make about yourself?
Values/Beliefs	Do you believe you can do it? Do you believe others believe in you? Does this fit in with what is important to you?
Capability	Have you been allowed to practise enough times and learn from your mistakes?
Behaviour	Have you been shown how to do it in a away that works for you? Visually, auditory, kinesthetically?
Environment	Is there enough of what you need? What is your inner state?

Environment: This includes the internal and the external environment. In our example, the mother's internal environment may be one of concern and worry. Externally life will be different now the baby has arrived, so there is the loss of the way life has been and adjustment to the way life has now become. All the externals will affect the internals and the internals will affect the externals.

Behaviour: The child is crying and at present the mother has not worked out the reason for this. She could see this as a behaviour issue and something with which she needs help, or as a behaviour issue that will work out in time as she becomes more practised. At worst, she can begin to see it as some sort of failure. Significant others around her at this point can often support her to see it as something that is just a matter of time and practice.

Significant others can also, consciously or unconsciously, feed the insecurity she is feeling. Comments that compare her or the baby to others are not helpful. Comments that highlight those aspects which she is worrying about, 'She's crying again', or 'Does she always cry this much?' are not helpful.

Capability: If the healthy route is chosen (by this I mean the route to a healthy self-esteem), then the mother will get to know her child and will learn motherhood, sometimes on her own and sometimes with the help of friends, extended family, health visitors, doctors or books. Some mothers need time and space to get to know their children and find themselves surrounded by helpers, which can cause the mother to feel she is in a goldfish bowl.

Some mothers will need to discuss what they are doing with lots of people to find agreement about what they are trying, some will watch and see, and others will need to feel right about it. These are the self-convincers. Some will require lots of time alone with the baby to try things out, some will need to phone someone constantly until they are sure and some will watch others.

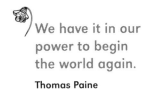 We have it in our power to begin the world again.

Thomas Paine

Beliefs and values: If the convincers have had time to work, then the belief will be a positive one, 'I can do this.' If the convincers have not, then the mother could believe she is a failure as a mother. The gap between the mother she sees herself to be and her ideal mother is so big and so inaccessible that her self-esteem as a mother is very low.

Identity: We build our identity from the beliefs we hold about how well we fit, function, are accepted and valued. We make the things we do and the responses we receive mean something about us. This means that the mother who has taken the healthy route may well end up having an identity statement about herself as a mother that is good, or at least good enough. The mother who has taken the not-so-healthy route may well have failure as a mother identity statement.

Spirituality: For many women the way through all the difficulties and joys of being a mother is very spiritual. It is based on the belief that we are here in this life to grow, to become closer to God, either God as a being without or God as an aspect within (sometimes both), and to be in service. Being a mother could be seen as the one opportunity we get to really be part of the miracle of creation. Therefore everything that happens to us as mothers is an opportunity to grow, learn, experience and choose how we respond – do we respond from fear or love? It is also a chance to go on being part of the creation of a different world, a world where people respond from love not fear. Modelling this can become the 'Noble Goal' we are working towards and mistakes along the way are not seen as something wrong, but as feedback to work on.

The ideal pupil

So how does this apply to the classroom? Where do children get their impression of the ideal pupil? They listen, watch and experience: they are checking out what the significant others, mainly adults when they are small, and often peers as they get older, are telling, showing or causing them to feel.

If we ask the children what makes an ideal pupil, they often come up with a list like this:

1   Stays on task.

2   Does not distract others.

3   Will have a go at new things.

4   Will have a go at answering questions.

5   Works well in a group/will get along with others.

6   Works well autonomously.

7   Enjoys learning.

If a child is very kinesthetic in her learning, lacks confidence in her ability, has undeveloped interpersonal or intrapersonal skills, she will fall very short of the above seven requirements. If each teacher that the child meets requires a different ideal pupil, then the child does not really stand a chance.

Remember Jason?

He had been taught to spell using phonics. He had found this very difficult and had soon been identified as having a spelling difficulty. Thereafter he was identified as having learning and behavioural difficulties. So let us look at how Jason may have created his identity statement and his level of self-esteem using the NLP Neurological Levels.

Environment: Jason had difficulty with learning to spell. He would have seen around him other children who seemed to be learning to spell more easily than he did. His internal environment may well have been a cause for concern; he was in a new place (school) and there were a lot of changes taking place for him.

Behaviour: This is the level at which Jason's notion of the ideal pupil began to develop. He, like the mother in the previous scenario, has a behaviour to deal with. Jason is not learning to spell in the way that is expected. He could see this as something he has not learned yet and look for alternative ways of learning. He could see it not as a fault in himself or anyone else, but simply as a series of trying new learning strategies and finding the ones that work. Or he could see it as a fault in himself – he is not good enough.

Jason is, at this point, a small child; he will take his lead from the significant adults around him.

What happens is that they try to teach him using phonics and this is very, very slow for him – it is his least preferred way of learning. So he has very little success in comparison to those he sees around him. However, instead of the adults experimenting with other modalities (visual or kinesthetic), they continue with the auditory, year after year, and Jason falls further and further behind. What is the message being given to Jason?

The message is not 'There is nothing wrong with you'. It is more likely to be 'Ideal Pupil = a child who could learn to spell phonetically'. If this were not so, why would the adults keep using the phonics, even though they are not helping at the rate they want? Conclusion: there is nothing wrong with our methods, they work for the majority = there must be something wrong with the child. Just like the mother in the previous scenario, Jason needs to be given the opportunity to become capable, able. He needs to feel able.

Capability: If the healthy route were chosen, then Jason would find out about himself as a learner. His difficulty in learning spelling in the same way as the other pupils would be a gift. He would now have an opportunity to get to know and understand his style of learning, he could find out about his self-convincers and how to spell in a way that works for him. He could develop as a writer, using what he had discovered about himself as a learner and taking that into other learning situations.

It took until Year 5 for this to happen. So in Years 1, 2, 3 and 4 Jason was not able to build up his capability. The ideal pupil was still the one who could spell, and added to that the ideal pupil was also one who:

1 Stays on task.

2 Doesn't distract others.

3 Will have a go at new things.

4 Will have a go at answering questions.

5 Works well in a group/ will get along with others.

6 Works well autonomously.

7 Enjoys learning.

Jason was a highly kinesthetic child. He needed to try things out, so often it looked as though he did not work well with others and was off task. His self-esteem was getting lower and so the likelihood of his trying new things became less. He did not have the confidence to work autonomously, particularly in written tasks. So he fell further behind the model of the ideal pupil.

Beliefs and values: If the convincers had been given a chance in the early years, then Jason could have had a positive belief about himself and would have seen his own value. However, by Year 5 he believed that he was unable to learn, he was difficult and stubborn, and no-one liked him.

Identity: The kind of identity statements we would like learners to have about themselves are:

- ❀ I am worthwhile.
- ❀ I count.
- ❀ I am smart.
- ❀ I am a successful learner.
- ❀ I am likeable.
- ❀ I can do things.
- ❀ I am capable.
- ❀ I can handle difficulties.
- ❀ I am perfect the way I am right now.
- ❀ I am strong.
- ❀ I am lovable.

Jason's identity statements were directly opposite to these by Year 5.

Spirituality: It would be wonderful if all children knew that they were perfect, beautiful creations, as we all are. But the ideal pupil is something that adults help to create for each pupil and we do it either consciously or unconsciously. It is very important for our young pupils that we do it very consciously. Otherwise we are having a deleterious effect on the self-esteem of our pupils.

It is no good praising a child for something he does not really believe you value. If he thinks the ideal pupil writes two pages and he has only written two lines, this is not praiseworthy in his eyes. If the ideal pupil sits still for the whole 20 minutes of literacy and he can only manage five, then this is also not praiseworthy in his eyes. If the ideal pupil can work autonomously without asking for help and he is constantly in need of help, he is not praiseworthy.

How do you support children in creating an ideal pupil that is a model to work towards but not an idealised creation that they can constantly use to feed negative identity statements? We shall look at identity in the next chapter.

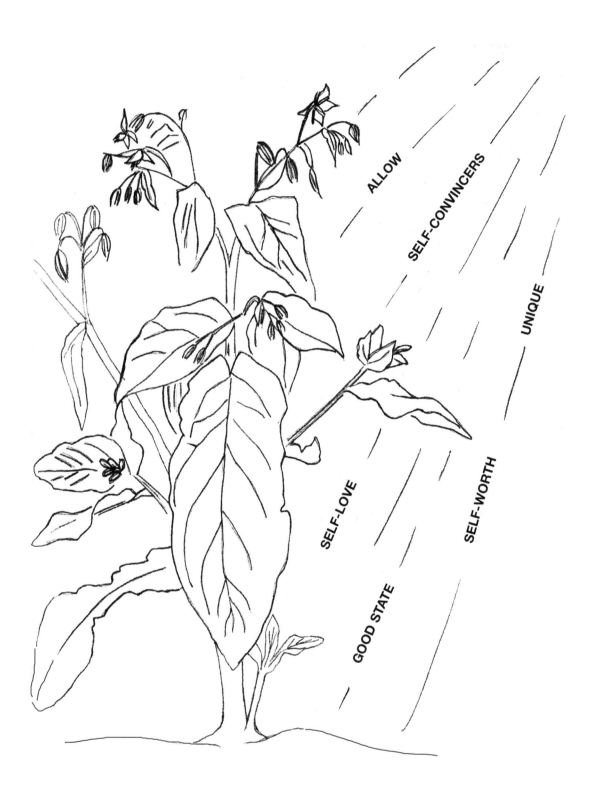

ALLOW

SELF-CONVINCERS

UNIQUE

SELF-LOVE

SELF-WORTH

GOOD STATE

Chapter 10

Creating identity: knowing myself and choosing who I am

'Who are you?' said the Caterpillar.

This was not an encouraging opening for a conversation.

Alice replied, rather shyly, 'I–I hardly know sir, just at present – at least I know who I was when I got up this morning, but I think I must have been changed several times since then.'

'What do you mean by that?' said the Caterpillar sternly. 'Explain yourself!'

Lewis Carroll[1]

The beliefs we hold about ourselves and the values we live by can create how we see our identity: the identity that we take on or that is given by others.

We make identity statements about ourselves, 'I'm artistic', 'I'm shy', 'I'm not mechanically minded', 'I'm very musical' – even 'I'm not loveable', 'I'm stupid', 'I'm ugly'. These statements have in many cases become who we are. Many of our identity statements are life enhancing and many are not. We have often taken a set of circumstances and created a meaning about them and then made it mean something about us.

 Some people say they haven't yet found themselves. But the self is not something one finds; it is something one creates.

Thomas Szasz

Sadly, if you look at the negative identity statements of a group of adults and trace such statements back to their origin, many of them will have started at school. The Neurological Levels model used by Neuro-Linguistic Programming (see page 109) is helpful in explaining how we often unconsciously cause children to take on negative identity statements. For example:

Environment

- ✿ A child in a class during literacy, sitting on the carpet for 15 minutes per day doing text and sentence/word work.

- ✿ No break states (changes in the state, that is, from listening to talking, from sitting still to moving, raising or lowering the energy).

Behaviour

- ✿ The child is sitting, listening and can see the text but not very well.

- ✿ The child is highly kinesthetic and auditory. Visual is his weakest mode.

- ✿ He keeps fidgeting and talking to the person next to him. The teacher has told him to stop being naughty and stop fidgeting; she says he must be good, sit still and listen not talk.

- ✿ The child needs to discuss the learning often after each piece, this is part of his auditory mode of learning, he also needs to move and experience. He finds it difficult to sit still at the moment. He likes to know the big picture and he is a lateral thinker and keeps coming up with all sorts of interesting off shoots from the text, which give it meaning to him and which he needs to discuss.

Capability

- ✿ The child is not finding it easy to take in information with predominantly visual stimulus.

- ✿ He is not being given the chance to develop this learning mode alongside the ones he is successful with.

- ✿ He is often getting it wrong and needs to move and talk thorough his connections; his teacher says he is very rude.

The child does not realise that he has a particular learning style and that he will need to develop other modalities, such as visual. He does not understand yet that moving around is just a part of the way he takes in the world and that there is nothing wrong with this, it is just distracting his teacher and maybe others. He also does not understand yet why he needs to discuss what he has heard and the connections he has made. He does not understand his learning style.

Beliefs and values

- ✿ He believes it is naughty not to sit still, it is normal to sit in silence and listen and that he should not have to discuss it. He believes it is rude to talk to the person next to him when he has an idea.

- ✿ He thinks he should be like the others: he should be able to sit still and to be silent and not speak for the whole of the time on the mat; yet he finds this impossible at the moment.

Identity

- ✿ When you talk to this child he tells you he is naughty (what other reason could there be) and he is stupid (he must be, other children can do it).

- ✿ He is rude otherwise he would be silent.

- ✿ He takes the feedback and makes it mean this about himself.

As teachers we are constantly communicating with children, giving them feedback about what they are doing. How careful are we?

- Do we consider children's learning modalities? (VAK)
- Do we consider their level of skill in the eight intelligences?
- Do we consider their thinking styles?
- Do we consider their level of self-esteem?
- Do we consider the three criteria for the 'knowing they know'?
- Do we inform them of their learning styles and what they need to develop?
- Do we consider the internal environment of a child?
- Do we know if a child is grieving, afraid, angry, sad?

Consider what negative statements you say about yourself: 'I'm not very artistic', 'I'm not mathematical', 'I'm not very practical', 'I haven't got green fingers', 'I'm not musical', 'I'm not good with numbers', 'I'm not creative'.

All that happened was no one found the correct learning style for you to learn these things and to feel successful at them.

You did, however, learn to do other things, which means when conditions are favourable you can learn and be successful.

Then there are the identity statements like: 'I'm shy', 'I'm thick', 'I'm slow', 'I'm annoying', 'I'm odd', 'I'm not likeable', 'I don't fit in'. These are built up as in my example above from adults not understanding the reasons children are behaving as they do and giving them messages that are then interpreted in a negative way.

A child who has a high level of intrapersonal skills may be someone who likes to watch and wait, who gives her contribution when she has checked it out internally, or she may need to discuss it with one or more people before she gives it.

This child could be labelled shy or slow.

The child whose learning modality is not being used can think he is being stupid. For example, if the teacher is very visual and lots of the class are as well, a kinesthetic learner (like myself) can feel very stupid. If I do not understand what criteria I need to help me 'know what I know', I can feel very thick. I need to practise a lot but only for a short period each time, then there comes a point when I feel I really know it. If I was given a long time, but only once or twice to practise something, I would not feel confident and would think I was thick.

The child above was led to believe he was annoying, rude, stupid and a fidget. How will this affect his self-image, self-esteem, motivation, confidence and ability to succeed?

How do we support children to build a positive identity and change it as they grow and develop?

 If we do not know what port we're steering for, no wind is favourable.

Seneca

Children need to:

- ❀ know themselves as learners, to understand how we learn and the differences in learning styles;

- ❀ understand their thinking styles so that they can develop them further;

- ❀ understand the different intelligences, which skills they have and which need to be developed;

- ❀ know their strengths in all areas including the above;

- ❀ know their personal qualities;

- ❀ know their skills including those above;

- ❀ know themselves in relationship to others;

- ❀ understand their uniqueness, value and potential;

- ❀ understand and take pride in their bodies;

- ❀ feel OK with the way they are right now;

- ❀ understand that change is possible and normal;

- ❀ develop awareness;

- ❀ understand that everyone's experience is unique;

- ❀ understand that experience differs according to whether they are male or female. It is affected by their cultural background, their physical appearance, the experiences life has given them so far;

- ❀ understand that as their awareness develops, so do the attitudes and interpretations they bring to each new experience;

- ❀ know that how they interpret experiences, what they will notice and how they notice it is dependent on them and how aware they are;

- ❀ understand that instead of having their identity given to them by others, they can constantly ask themselves 'who am I?' and 'who am I becoming?'.

Working with children and supporting them to look at themselves can make a great difference to *their levels of motivation, self-esteem and learning success, their sense of belonging, capability and value.*

As the children become more aware of themselves and of those around them, they begin to feel safer and to see themselves as unique individuals who are 'work in progress'.

Exercises to support the development of identity

 If you cannot find it in yourself, where will you go for it?

Chinese proverb

The following exercises are designed to help you to understand more about the identity you have created so far. They can also be done with children to develop their self-awareness.

Will the real xxx please stand up!!

This exercise allows us to see how much of ourselves we are willing to share with others.

Exercise

1 Use a sheet with concentric rings and label them:

   ✽ strangers (outer ring)

   ✽ people I know, parents, friends, close friends, partner, myself (inner circle)

2 Ask yourself some questions – who would you tell:

   ✽ Your favourite movie?

   ✽ The most embarrassing thing that has happened to you?

   ✽ What you dislike most about your body?

   ✽ What makes you cry?

   ✽ What is the most important thing in your life?

   ✽ If you could change one thing about the world, what would it be?

3 If you are doing this alone spend some time looking at who you are willing to share the inner you with.

It is very important that there is no judgement made about the levels of privacy people choose. So if you are doing this activity alone, do not judge yourself, and if you are doing it with a group of adults or children, it is important to have first set ground rules or agreements. The point of the activity is only to raise each individual's awareness of themselves.

You may have thought you were very open and see that in fact you are not.

Until you are aware of the present, you are not able to *choose* to be different or *choose* to stay the same.

Generally the levels of privacy we have are there because of circumstances in our lives. Those circumstances change and the factors that have caused us to be very private or very open may have changed. However, we may still be reacting to old attitudes out of habit, and they may have become automatic behaviours, part of our identity. When we look at the results of this activity we may choose to open up a bit more or become a bit more private. We now have conscious choice about it instead of its being a reaction to circumstances.

Our life as a journey

One of the most important aspects of Emotional Intelligence is the ability to see your life as a journey of growth, development and choices. Life happens and we often have no conscious control over what happens to us; however, we do have a choice about how we interpret it, what we make it mean, or who we will be in response to it.

Children or adults can do this activity: you look at your life so far as a journey and draw it in whatever way you like.

Exercise

1 Take your time and think about how best you can represent your life on the page. Think about the ups and the downs, the turning points, the crossroads and the forks in the road.

2 If you need to talk to someone about the journey first, then do. When you are ready, draw the journey of your life so far.

3 Now look at the drawing and ask yourself the following questions (you can do this with a partner of your choice):

❀ What has your journey been like?

❀ What have the 'ups' taught you?

❀ What have the 'downs' taught you?

❀ What has supported you so far on your journey?

❊ What do you need to support you for the next part?

❊ Where is your journey leading?

❊ What have been the major turning points?

❊ What have been the major lessons?

If the exercises are done in groups, then the following ground rules are needed:

❊ People are free to choose any partner with whom they feel comfortable.

❊ No one refuses to listen to anyone who brings their drawing to share with them.

❊ If someone chooses you to share their journey with, you do not have to share yours with them.

❊ Listen sensitively to people's stories.

❊ When you have listened to their story, find someone with whom to share your story.

❊ If you do not want to share your story, then you do not have to.

❊ You may prefer to spend time on your own reflecting on your journey.

Inside outside

 Each of us is meant to have a character all our own, to be what no other can exactly be, and do what no other can exactly do.

William Ellery Channing

Another exercise that helps us reflect on ourselves is looking at 'the me I show to the world' and 'the me inside'.

Exercise

1 Take a sheet of A3 paper and fold it in half.

2 On one half draw a representation of 'me on the outside' (crayons are very useful for this); on the other side draw 'me on the inside.'

3 As with the life journey activity opposite, the drawings can be shared with a partner using the same ground rules.

Some people see that the inside picture and the outside picture are very similar, while for others they are very different.

Who am I becoming?

This is a variation on aspiration posters.

Exercise

1 Ask yourself, 'who would you love to become?'

2 Use all the modalities and remember the sky's the limit:

❊ What would you look like?

❊ What would you sound like?

❀ What would you be doing?

❀ What would you be feeling?

❀ What sort of qualities would you have?

❀ What sort of skills would you have?

❀ What sort of gifts would you have?

3 You can create the poster as a collage, a 3D model, a poem.

4 When you have created the aspiration poster/model, it can be on display somewhere that is useful to you.

One way of using the aspiration poster/model to change behaviour in the present is to ask yourself or the pupil, 'If I were that person right now, what would I do?'

This is a wonderful tool for change if used well. It is one I have used on myself for many years. I usually create a collage (being kinesthetic that suits me); the collage contains images and words that represent the 'me' I am becoming and the 'me' I aspire to. When it is complete, I show it to several people whom I trust to support me and explain it to them. I then put it on my bedroom wall.

Even though making the poster can have an effect by itself, the effect is very limited. The power of this activity is in how you use the poster.

Every time you have a choice to make you think of the poster and say to yourself, 'What would she do?' You then act accordingly. Each time you do that you have become her. The more you do it, the more you become the person you aspire to be. When I feel I have become the person in my poster, I do a new one.

> Vision isn't enough unless combined with venture. It's not enough to stare up the steps unless we also step up the stairs.
>
> **Vance Havner**

Children often show themselves surrounded with friends, having lots of fun. When they behave in ways that are 'anti-social', you can get them to look at the poster and ask what would she do in this situation? What choices would she make? In this exercise we only need to pretend, pretend to be that person whom we aspire to be and soon we will be. This is all intrinsic motivation based on the person I wish to be.

Case study: Karen's story

Karen, a girl I was supporting a few years ago, is a good example of the concept that we choose how we interpret the things that happen to us. She was in Year 7 in the top year of middle school.

The reasons I had been asked to see her were: she was having difficulty concentrating on work; she was arguing a great deal with lots of the children in her class; her work was deteriorating; and she had run away one afternoon after school and had not been found until 9 p.m. that evening.

In the first session with her we got to know each other and she told me about her family and how her father had left her mother before she was even born, 'He has never even seen me.' She added that no one in her class liked her, she had no friends and gave several more details about her life.

In the second session she came in a very distressed state. She said she had been having a very bad day and the boys in her class were teasing her. She asked, 'Why Miss? Why did all this happen to me? Why did my father leave me without even seeing me? Why do the children in my class not like me? Why does my mum not understand me?'

There were lots of answers I could have given to those questions, but the one I gave is based on there being many interpretations to any situation. I replied, 'What if the reason all this has happened is because you are a very special person?'

She looked stunned and went very quiet. I could see her work the question through and then she said, 'Well, that would mean I had to learn something from it all.'

I asked her what had she learned and she replied, 'I have a lot of love in me and a lot of understanding. I'm compassionate, Miss, you know, and people come to me and talk to me, and I listen and I understand what they mean.'

Then she said, 'We've been doing stuff on optimism and pessimism in class, and I suppose that I could look at it from the optimist's chair or the pessimist's chair.' I agreed with her – and now I was the one who was stunned.

The third and final time she came to see me, she got two chairs out. She sat in one and had a real moan about her week, and then sat in the other and said what she had learned from her week.

The last thing we did on that third session was to make a list. I asked her, 'If you were advertising yourself as a friend and trying to really sell yourself, what would you say?'

The list she wrote was amazing:

* I am a great listener even when I am fed up, because I know what it is like to really need someone to listen.
* I am not too pretty so the boys will notice you first, probably, but I am pretty enough not to put them off.
* I am very loyal and will always stand by you no matter what.
* If you are feeling depressed, I can help you to look at the optimistic side of things.
* I know how it feels to feel alone.
* I have a great sense of humour.

❀ I love pop music and dancing.

❀ I'd love to have sleepovers and drink hot chocolate and chat all night.

❀ Most of all I would be your friend for life if you wanted.

She looked at the list, smiled and said, 'I'd choose me as a friend.'

This child is still in touch with me and writes to tell me how she is doing in secondary school (and she is doing really well, when potentially she was going in the direction of dropping out), which boys she fancies and about her very special friend.

She taught me so much: about how easy children find this work and how willing they are to take responsibility for their lives and give up the victim role. Also how willing they are to choose who they want to be and go for it. When we allow them to be as great as they truly are and support them on their journey, then they become greater than we could have ever imagined.

Supporting each other's growing identity

 We meet ourselves time and again in a thousand disguises on the paths of life.

Carl Jung

As we change our identity and become the person we really choose to be, we start noticing that everyone around us begins to change. I am speaking here from personal experience and from the experience of many friends and colleagues who have reported the same phenomenon.

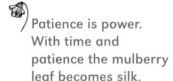 Patience is power. With time and patience the mulberry leaf becomes silk.

Chinese proverb

There is a very short exercise you can do to see the difference this makes to you and others around you.

Exercise

1 Pretend you are already the person you would choose to be. Who would that person see when they looked out at all those around them?

2 At a certain point each day start noting down the positive things you have noticed in the people you have dealt with that day.

   a) What did they do?

   b) What did they say?

   c) How did it feel being around them?

3 How has each person you have met today contributed to you?

If you are doing the same work with children in a group, the following exercise is one way of their noticing and supporting each other's growth and development. It gives members of the class a chance to share positive statements about each other and take away a visual symbol of how they are seen in the class group.

The emphasis is on *individual's qualities, abilities or skills, those attributes that are special or unique to them,* and the part played by the class is to *identify those qualities in each other.*

This exercise needs to be done with a group who know each other fairly well. Doing it some time after doing the aspiration posters is good and can be used as a way of noticing the development of qualities, abilities or skills the children have aspired to.

The children work in groups, maybe the groups with whom they did the aspiration posters.

Exercise

1 Give out large sheets of plain paper and make sure a variety of coloured pens or crayons is available to each group.

2 The children take their sheet of paper and *draw around the outline of their hand*, making sure it is in the centre of the paper. They then take a few minutes colouring in the drawing in a way that represents them and how they are feeling. They put their name somewhere on the drawing.

3 The children think of the others in the group. How have they helped them? What quality do they like about them? What are their strong points? Have they noticed any positive qualities developing recently?

4 Then in their small groups ask them to look at each other's drawings and *write down on each person's drawing something they like about that person.*

5 They can sign their name at the end of the comment. They might want to say something about *a skill they admire*, or *something the person has done or said,* something they have developed, or any positive comment that comes to mind.

6 When they have finished everyone in their group, they might like to walk around the room and add positive comments to the drawings of people in other groups.

7 They then need to take their drawing, read the comments on it and talk about the drawing and the comments with the other members of the small group.

Giving and receiving gifts

This is a way of recognising someone's hopes and aspirations and what support they might need in their journey towards them.

This exercise can be linked to the aspiration posters and the children can share their posters with a partner or small group. Then the partner or group decide what gift the person could receive which would help them achieve their aspirations.

Emphasise the importance of choosing something positive that their partner would appreciate and that material goods are not always the gifts we value the most.

Exercise

1 Each person considers what they know about their partner and writes down or draws the gift the partner would like to receive.

2 Now they exchange their gifts and explain why they chose that particular gift for their partner.

3 Then the group swap and everyone gets a new partner and does the process again. This can continue until the group have all partnered each other. The group can come together at the end and discuss the following:

❀ What were the gifts you received?

❀ How did if feel to receive gifts?

❀ Which did you like most and why?

❀ How did it feel to give gifts?

❀ How did you choose what to give?

Giving and receiving gifts that are not material is not something most people are used to. The above exercise is placed in this chapter because I feel it is so important to notice how each person is growing and developing and to feed and nurture, not destroy. If children do these exercises and the others in this book, the difference in schools could be enormous.

If we could see each person we come across as another flower in the garden with us, a different flower maybe but still a flower. Each flower wants to fully express its beauty, colour, fragrance and gift. We are all at different stages of growth, yet if we look at every person around us and see them as a beautiful flower that may not yet have bloomed, we could then ask ourselves, 'What gift could I give this person that would support their growth?' It might be a smile, or a word or two of recognition or encouragement, or even a thought or a silent blessing. Try this out with those around you and watch and note down what happens.

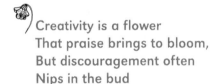

Creativity is a flower
That praise brings to bloom,
But discouragement often
Nips in the bud

Alex F. Osborn

Imagine seeing a dark cave
With a large and luminous flower
Floating in the darkness,
Shining with the light of inner wisdom.
The flower remains hidden, for it doesn't appreciate its own beauty, and in revealing itself,
In opening to the light it fears it might be destroyed.
In what ways might you be like that flower?
Do you invite others into your private spaces?
What if you trusted enough to come out of the cave,
To reveal your heart, your vulnerability
Your own inner light?

Dan Millman[2]

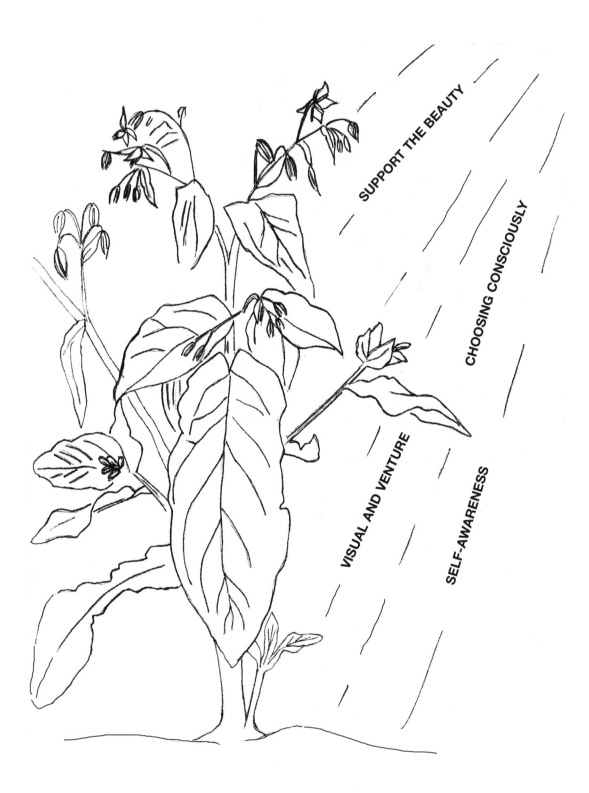

SUPPORT THE BEAUTY

CHOOSING CONSCIOUSLY

VISUAL AND VENTURE

SELF-AWARENESS

Becoming Emotionally Intelligent – Catherine Corrie

Chapter 11

Optimism and pessimism: their effects on learning

 I have made my world and it is a much better world than I ever saw outside.

Louise Nevelson

Optimism is a learned behaviour. It can be taught and have a massive effect on how we interpret our environment, how we respond emotionally and how we behave. It is important to support children to become resilient and courageous in the face of adversity, failure and mistakes.

Adversity, Failure and Mistakes

The pessimistic state

People living in a pessimistic state view these three conditions as **permanent**. This means that their internal negative dialogue is being constantly reinforced: 'I am a Failure', 'I'm *never* going to get through this. As soon as I come up, life knocks me down again.'

These conditions are also seen as **global**: 'Why does this *always* happen to me?', 'I *can't ever* get it right', '*Everyone* is out to get me'.

The optimistic state

People in an optimistic state, however, view the three conditions as **temporary**: 'I haven't managed it *yet*', 'I'll do better *next time*'.

These conditions are also seen as **specific**: 'I have difficulty with spelling, and the content of my writing is good', 'At the moment I am having a lot of difficulties in my relationship', 'There are a few people who seem to be sabotaging my efforts'.

The pessimistic state	The optimistic state
Lastly, they are interpreted as their owner having **no ability**: 'I'm stupid', 'I'm hopeless'.	Optimists view difficult situations as **lacking in something** – something specific was not done: 'I didn't get enough visual input to really know it', 'I need to practise more', 'I need to get a better relationship with ....'
	Lastly, these situations are perceived as **opportunities to learn and grow**: 'Next time I will remember to practise more', 'That was caused by a breakdown in communication; I will communicate more clearly in future', 'I have noticed how easily I give up; I need to get support to change that pattern'.
	It is also important for children to recognise and take credit for Success, Achievement, and Fortune.

Success, Achievement and Fortune

The pessimistic state	The optimistic state
The pessimist will perceive these three conditions to be **temporary**: 'but I won't be able to do it again'.	The optimist, on the other hand, perceives these successful states as permanent: 'I can do this', 'I've learned five tunes now'.
They will view them as **specific**: 'I am rubbish at maths, that was just adding.'	Also they see them as **global**: 'I can play the piano', ' I can read', ' I am capable'.
Lastly, they see them as **accidental**: 'I don't know how that happened', 'It was just a fluke', 'I only won because everyone else was so bad', 'They probably lowered the pass mark'.	Lastly, they view them as **due to hard work or effort**: 'I really did well!', 'I earned that'.

> What doesn't kill me makes me stronger
>
> **Albert Camus**

As these tables show, there is no such thing as a pessimist or an optimist, there is only pessimistic and optimistic thinking. It simply depends how we view situations.

Case study: Olivia's story

My daughter normally has very optimistic thinking. She is an actress and learned very early on in her career that auditioning and being turned down for a role was part of the job. Yet recently she auditioned for a very nice part in a short film and when I phoned her three hours after the audition she was in a very pessimistic state. The studio had said they would call back the people they liked for a second audition by a certain time, that time had now passed and she had not been called. She was in a pessimistic state because she was now putting this into *permanent*, *global* and *no ability*, 'I can't act, I should choose another career. What is wrong with me? I'm obviously hopeless, not even a call back.'

Fifteen minutes later she was in optimistic thinking, 'It's been a while since my last audition and I felt really out of practice. This made me much more nervous than usual. I must try and make sure I have regular acting practice.' She talked about a part in a play (unpaid) she would go for as it would be fun and keep her in practice.

Ten minutes after that conversation the studio called her back for a second audition. She laughed when I saw her and said, 'I don't believe what I did on Saturday, I got myself into a right state.'

She is correct – she got herself into the state. Life happens to us as I have said in previous chapters and we have a choice about how we interpret it.

> In the middle of difficulty lies opportunity.
> **Albert Einstein**

If we think *permanent*, *global* and *no ability* when we make mistakes or fail at something, then we are thinking pessimistically and, if you think back to the section on victims, this causes us to go into victim role. Victim role and pessimistic thinking have no power to change anything. So the circumstance will very likely persist.

As teachers this knowledge and understanding is very important. Some pupils have become habitual pessimistic thinkers even at a very early age, and this is usually modelled from a significant other. Pupils' self-esteem is also affected by this thinking because it will not allow success to be permanent. If a pupil does succeed or achieve, the pessimistic thinking will make it *temporary, specific* or *accidental*. You will hear comments such as 'it was just a fluke', 'yes, well I won't be able to do it again' or 'that was last time, this time it's different'. The person thinking this way when they have achieved well is not allowing it to become a permanent part of their development.

> I shall become master in this art only after a great deal of practice.
> **Erich Fromm**

The section below describes a simple way of changing pessimistic thinking into optimistic thinking – you simply change the words. The pessimistic thoughts will be connected to feelings and emotions and these will often be hopeless, helpless, shameful emotions, which as I have explained previously are emotions we fear, causing flight, fight, freeze or flock reactions. If we change the thoughts, we also change the emotions and so we change the reactions.

Use of language

Trust that still small voice that says, 'this might work and I'll try it.'

Diane Mariechild

We can change negative self-talk and pessimistic self-talk into positive and optimistic self-talk by using positive presuppositions; for example '*when I have mastered* these sums, I am moving on to the next level', the 'when I have mastered' presupposes that you will ('*when I have passed* my driving test, I will take a trip to Brighton').

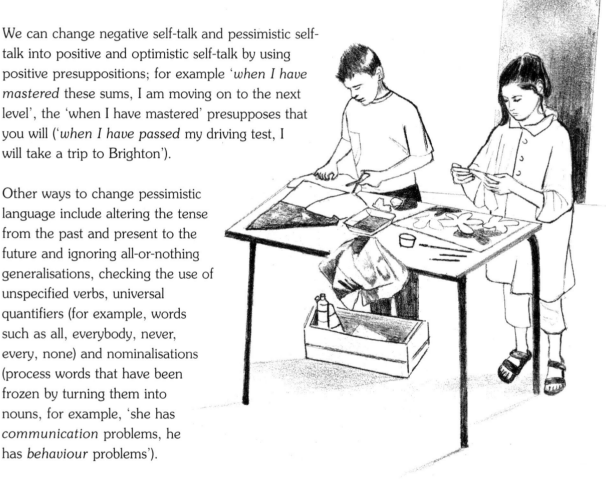

Other ways to change pessimistic language include altering the tense from the past and present to the future and ignoring all-or-nothing generalisations, checking the use of unspecified verbs, universal quantifiers (for example, words such as all, everybody, never, every, none) and nominalisations (process words that have been frozen by turning them into nouns, for example, 'she has *communication* problems, he has *behaviour* problems').

These are some very simple ways to change pessimistic language. If you use these yourself and begin to model them when you are around other people, you will be amazed at the effect. Just try out a simple one now as you read this.

Exercise

1 Think of something you feel hopeless at or just cannot do.
2 Say to yourself 'I can't do it, I can't do, I can't do it.'
3 Notice how you feel.
4 Now say to yourself 'I can't do it yet, that is true, I can't do it yet.'
5 Notice how that feels.

Words that cause you to be stuck	Words that open possibility
No	= Not yet
Never	= When I'm ready
I can't	= I can, though I can't yet
I'm no good at xx	= I'm really getting better at xx
I don't want to be different	= I don't need to be the same
No one likes me	= Sharon is my friend
I got a low score	= I'll do better next time
I'm stuck	= I'll move on and come back to it
I'm uncomfortable	– About what? About whom?
They don't listen to me	– Who specifically doesn't listen?
They hate me	– Who specifically hates you?
It's better to leave it	– Better than what?
She makes me angry	– How exactly does she do that?
She never listens to me	– Never? What happens when she does? What would happen if she did?
She's always telling me off. She hates me	– Have you ever told off someone you liked? What if her telling you off means she likes you?

> We learn to do something by doing it. There is no other way.
>
> **John Holt**

If we think pessimistically, we make our failure or difficulties feel and sound permanent, global, or as if we have no ability; for example, the statements below seem fixed and permanent.

I'm hopeless at maths	Permanent
They never listen to me	*They* implies loads of people or everyone and *never* implies without exception.
I never get it right	Permanent – never have, never will.
I have spelling problems	Spelling is a process, but the pessimist perceives spelling problems as a something, like a noun.

| If only I was smart like them then I could … | Pre-supposition that they are smart and you are not, or that being smart is what is needed. |
| I always hit the wrong notes. I am tone deaf | Two things which do not go together. Hitting the wrong note could have lots of causes, so why pick that one? |

The above thoughts have emotional responses connected with them. As I have mentioned previously these sorts of feeling do not usually cause responses that are conducive to learning.

One way to change pessimistic thinking is to use the optimistic framework. In the face of difficulty, failure or mistakes, we need to teach the children to incorporate optimistic thinking. In other words, to view the problem as temporary, specific and that something is lacking. For example:

I'm hopeless at maths	Which specific part of it do you find difficult? Give them support. Try that bit on your own now.
They never listen to me	Who, specifically, doesn't listen? Never? Without exception? What would it take, do you think, to get them to listen? What would it be like if they listened?
I never get it right	You haven't got it right yet? What will it be like when you do? Let's see what it would take for you to be able to do it. What do you think is missing in the way you're being taught?
I have spelling problems	How would you like to spell better? Which words would you like to learn first? So what method have you used to learn? We could try a visual/auditory/kinesthetic learning method.
If only I was smart like them, then I could xx	But you are smart, just think you can xx. It isn't about being smart, it's about practice. You could if you practised enough. How do you think they got to be good at that?

I always hit the wrong notes. I'm tone deaf	How does hitting the wrong note mean you are tone deaf? Do you ever hit the right note? Maybe you just need some help in knowing where to place the notes inside your body. Hitting the wrong notes is often due to tension.

To support children, yourself or colleagues through changing pessimistic thoughts to optimistic thoughts when difficulty, failure or mistakes happen, remember it is *temporary, specific* and *something's lacking!*

We also need to use this process when success, achievement and fortune happens. We want them to think *permanent, global, hard work, effort, successful learning.*

> Learning is movement from moment to moment.
>
> J. Krishnamurti

So we need to use appropriate language. Here are some examples:

- ❧ You are so capable.
- ❧ The way you did that was fantastic
- ❧ When you practise enough see how well you do.
- ❧ Now that you have found the key to learning that, there'll be no stopping you.
- ❧ Now you have balance you'll be speed cycling soon.
- ❧ Every time you take your time you get it right.

This sort of language is *permanent, global* and *takes account of effort and learning.*

The emotional response to this language is very different and enhances learning and a feeling of success and optimism.

LANGUAGE

RESILIENT

COURAGEOUS

POSSIBILITY

Becoming Emotionally Intelligent – Catherine Corrie

Chapter 12

Spirituality and spiritual intelligence

Each one of us will interpret 'spirit' in our own way. It has to do with that which endures. It expresses itself in hope, compassion, thankfulness, courage, a sense of well-being and peace. It is closely related to that which gives purpose and meaning to our lives.

Values and Visions[1]

Neither IQ nor EQ, separately or in combination, is enough to explain the full complexity of human intelligence nor the vast richness of the human soul and imagination. Computers have high IQ: they know what the rules are and can follow them without making mistakes. Animals often have high EQ: they have a sense of the situation they are in and know how to respond appropriately. But neither computers nor animals ask why we have these rules or this situation, or whether either could be different or better ...

It is in its transformative power that SQ [spiritual intelligence] differs mainly from EQ ... my spiritual intelligence allows me to ask if I want to be in this particular situation in the first place. Would I rather change the situation, creating a new one?

Zohar and Marshall[2]

To be able to make sense of our experience we need to be able to reflect and contemplate. To do this we need to be able to 'move beyond' or 'rise above' the boundaries of the situation we are in, and neither logic nor Emotional Intelligence alone will enable this to happen. By using only IQ and EQ all we can do is make the best of the situation, to be able to see it clearly. To be able to see beyond it, however, we need another type of intelligence.

In her book *Spiritual Intelligence*, Danah Zohar[2] discusses the three neural networks in the brain. IQ is based on 'serial neural wiring' and EQ is based on 'associative neural wiring'. Zohar points out that if these are all the functions we have available, 'Neither reason nor emotions can appeal to anything beyond themselves.' SQ is based on the brain's third neural system, the 'synchronous neural oscillations' that unify data across the whole brain. This system allows a dialogue between *reason* and *emotion*, between *mind* and *body*. It allows for *growth* and *transformation*.

> If you stop for a moment and listen to your thoughts ... who is listening?
>
> **Anon**

Chapter 11 examined the creation of the identity; if this identity is only the result of being moulded by what has happened to us, then we have no choice about who we become.

I believe that when we enact the role of victim, persecutor or rescuer, we are reacting within that boundary. Everything is happening to us and we blame, feel sorry for ourselves or try our best to fix it. When we step beyond this way of thinking and say to ourselves 'what am I doing here?', 'what do I want from this situation?' or 'what have I learned from that situation?', then we have used what Zohar would call SQ, or what could be termed wisdom.

Many of the ideas within this book are ways of developing not only Emotional Intelligence but also Emotional Wisdom, or Spiritual Intelligence.

Our logical mind and IQ can only work with what it already knows, within the boundaries of logic. Our emotional mind and EQ can tell us how we feel about things and how best to react to a situation. Our unified mind, wisdom and SQ can 'step back' or 'rise above' the situation and behave creatively, with vision and flexibility to 'rewire' the person we are and become more, to grow and transform ourselves into the highest vision we can create ourselves to be.

To develop Emotional Wisdom we need to work on the following:

- ❀ Listening to our inner voice, our intuition, not our ramblings.

- ❀ Being responsible for how we interpret and react to everything that happens to us and everything we do.

- ❀ Choosing that which is in line with our highest values.

- ❀ Being responsible for breaking behaviour patterns that are not supporting our growth and development.

- ❀ Noticing when we are judging ourselves and others and reminding ourselves that *everyone* is perfect and their behaviour just reflects the fact they have forgotten that.

- ❀ Developing the capacity to be flexible (actively and spontaneously adapt).
- ❀ Developing self-awareness.
- ❀ Being able to use suffering as a way of getting stronger.
- ❀ Being able to feel the pain and do it anyway.
- ❀ The quality of being inspired by vision and values.
- ❀ The quality of harmlessness.
- ❀ Being able to see the connection between diverse things (being holistic).
- ❀ Asking 'why?' and 'what if?' questions and seeking 'fundamental' answers.
- ❀ Being able to work against convention when necessary.
- ❀ Working towards every action we take being for the highest good of all (would we pray for rain in a dry season even if our roof were leaking?).

If we are to evolve as human beings, then we have to develop this area of our intelligence. In the Western world today we are in a spiritual desert where materialism, expediency, self-centredness and the 'god money' seem to reign. There is a general lack of meaning in people's lives, a feeling of 'what's the point'.

Recently I ran a training day with a group of NQTs who had been teaching for two terms. At the beginning of the session I ask them to mill around and introduce themselves to each other, and to say *what two things they had enjoyed the most about their first two terms as teachers*. I was saddened by how many said the holidays as one of the two things they had enjoyed the most and by the lack of inspiration they seemed to feel.

Teaching is a job for people with vision. It is hard work mentally, physically and emotionally and if all we bring to it is our IQ, or even our EQ, the best we can do is survive, be a good role model and stay sane (and live from holiday to holiday).

To do more for the world than the world does for you – that is success.

Henry Ford

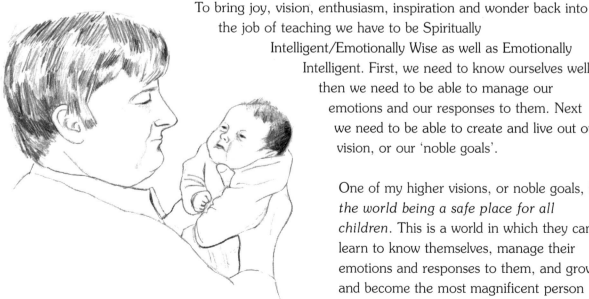

To bring joy, vision, enthusiasm, inspiration and wonder back into the job of teaching we have to be Spiritually Intelligent/Emotionally Wise as well as Emotionally Intelligent. First, we need to know ourselves well, then we need to be able to manage our emotions and our responses to them. Next we need to be able to create and live out our vision, or our 'noble goals'.

One of my higher visions, or noble goals, is *the world being a safe place for all children*. This is a world in which they can learn to know themselves, manage their emotions and responses to them, and grow and become the most magnificent person their minds can imagine. This goal is the cause of just about every action I take. It is the reason a woman who has always believed she cannot write has found the courage to write this book. The belief that it will make a difference.

Children are often way ahead of us in SQ: they are spontaneous, imaginative, visionary and they constantly ask 'why?' and 'what if?'

Case study: the Earth in space

I recently observed a lesson in a primary school Year 4 class, it was a science lesson and the first in a series of sessions on the Earth in space. The teacher was a trainee and she was brilliant. First, she did a visualisation with the children in which she asked them to imagine they were in a space ship and could see the planet from space. They were to look out and notice the size, colour and shape of each planet and could name them. When they opened their eyes they had a large blank sheet and they could draw, write and explain what they had seen.

Then in their groups they discussed what they would like to know about what they had seen. The questions were amazing: 'Why are there planets and why are they all different?', 'How long will the Sun last before it burns out?', 'How did God imagine something so fantastic?', 'Why have no other planets we see got people on them?'

The questions went on and on and I remember thinking, 'Adults would never ask such interesting questions, we have been conditioned not to wonder.'

Children do not worry about convention and when supported they can use their painful experiences to grow.

Case study: Martin's story

I was once teaching a class of Year 6 students when one of the Year 6 boys died. This experience more than anything else in my teaching career taught me how amazing children are if they are just allowed to be.

The 59 children who were in the year group were devastated when they found out that Martin was dying. They were all very used to doing circle time, as this was a school where children had space to find out about themselves and others in a very safe way.

We put them into circles when we told them the news and a week later when Martin had died. The children cried, sobbed, got angry, some allowed themselves to break-down completely. They also hugged and rocked each other, said 'It's OK we'll get through this together', and after a whole day of crying they began to talk to me and ask me questions:

✿ Where has Martin gone?

✿ Why him?

✿ Will we still be able to speak to him?

✿ What is the point of his death?

✿ Why couldn't God make him better? And lots more.

They asked questions about the funeral and wanted to write some poems. They made a memory book with photos, stories and poems for Martin's parents. They created a shrine to Martin's memory and at the funeral two of them read out the most beautiful and moving poems I have ever heard about the gift Martin had been to them and how much they had learned from his life and from his death.

Around the grave when the adults had gone, they sat and talked to each other and to Martin, again remembering the gift he had been and still was being.

As the rest of the year went by, they never forgot and Martin's memory shrine became a memorial garden in the school.

Those children allowed the emotions, the pain, the learning and the growth. They have been some of the greatest teachers I have ever had.

Children start with an advantage and often we as adults squash their natural spirit and Spiritual Intelligence. They look at the world and wonder, they ask the questions we have forgotten to ask and they dare to see themselves as wonderful and amazing until we tell them they are not.

The vision I hold is one where all children can feel it is OK to be them, where their potential is recognised, where their vision is supported, where they can grow and develop to become the greatest beings that they can imagine themselves to be, and where they can contribute and give of themselves to those around them.

This vision is what gets me out of bed, is what causes me to do the work I do, is why I wrote this book, is what brings joy, purpose and meaning to my life, and is where I go to when I want to check the situations I find myself in. If a course I was asked to run was not in line with my vision, I would simply not do it. If the publishers of this book had not had a similar vision for children, I would have found it very difficult to work with them on this. I had to overcome lots of emotional and logical blocks to produce this book. If I had relied on logic, I would have said I did not have the skills necessary to write a book. If I had gone to my emotions, then fear would have been very difficult to overcome due to a lifetime as a dyslexic who was told she could not write. But my vision for children, creating every school as a 'People Place', is what kept me going each time I froze at the computer.

As teachers or adults who work with children ask yourself, 'What is your vision and are you living it?' When you check your responses, keep the thoughts and actions that are

in line with your vision and discard and replace those that are not. Take each day one step at a time. If you know that some of your actions are not in keeping with your highest vision, then use your Spiritual Intelligence to imagine yourself differently.

Recently I have had several teachers tell me about the amazing results they noticed when they changed their thoughts about a child. After completing the exercise to write down the first thought about a child that comes into your head (see page 25), one very sceptical woman was transformed and kept saying 'It's like magic. I just found a new and more growthful thought and the boy changed in a couple of weeks … he was allowed to become that which he already was.' One small step and she has probably changed a child's life.

One of the great tragedies of our time is the death of the imagination – because what else is paralysis?

> I believe that the imagination is the passport we create to take us into the real world. It is another phrase for what is most uniquely us. To face ourselves. That's the hard thing. The imagination is God's gift to make the act of self-examination bearable. It teaches us our limits and how to grow beyond our limits … the imagination is the place we are all trying to get to.
>
> John Guare[3]

Every time we go beyond the boundaries of our logical minds and imagine ourselves to be more than we are being at present, we allow the possibility for growth. Then if we begin to live into that vision of ourselves, pretend to be it already, check our thoughts, our words and our actions against that vision and begin to be more in line with it, we become it: we become the selves of our imaginations, we become that which we are pretending, simply because it is true in the first place.

> It is never too late to be what we might have been.
>
> **George Eliot**

Another way of raising our Spiritual Intelligence is the ability to learn and grow from painful experiences, or adversity. Here is one example of how easily children do this; it is the case study from Chapter 10. I use it here to reinforce the point that we can learn to grow from painful experiences.

When a young girl first came to see me she told me all about how hard her life had been, and that her father had left her mother before she was even born. She said he must have hated her and didn't even want to see her. I did many different things with her which supported her seeing beyond and rising above the circumstances, thus she could see the full picture and go beyond just her own emotional responses to it.

But one thing we did together really changed her life in an instant. One day she said to me, '*Why? Why did this have to happen to me?*' And I asked her a question, '*If it happened because you are special and you needed to learn something what would that something be?*'

She stopped and thought, and her face changed before my eyes. She said, 'Well, I have learned compassion, I understand other people's pain and I listen to them, and never tell them not to be so silly. I have a very big heart.' From then on we used to look at all her 'problems' in the context of what she learned from them.

I hope that this book helps you to know yourself, choose yourself, become the vision of yourself you choose and give yourself joyfully to your families, friends, jobs, local and global communities.

Here is a tribute that was adapted and read by a friend of mine, Ian Berry (a teacher), for a friend and colleague at his funeral. Many of us are teachers whether in the formal or informal sense, and the important thing is to choose it consciously, to love it, to value it and to grow from it.

We are teachers

We are teachers

We are born the first moment that a question leaped from the mouth of a child.

We have been many people in many places.

We were Socrates inspiring the youth of Athens to discover new ideas through the use of questions.

We were Ann Sullivan tapping out the secrets of the universe into the outstretched hand of Helen Keller.

We were Aesop, Hans Christian Andersen and the Brothers Grimm, revealing wisdom through their countless stories.

The name of those who have practised our profession ring like a clear bell of wisdom sounding out for humanity.

Buddha, Confucius, Christ,

Dewey, Steiner, Montessori,

Plato, Aristotle, Moses, Mohammed.

We are also those whose names and faces have long been forgotten but whose lessons and whose character will always be remembered in the accomplishments of their students.

We have wept for joy at the weddings of former students, glowed with a knowing pride at the birth of their child. Some of us have bowed our heads in grief and confusion beside graves dug too soon for bodies far too young.

Throughout the course of a day we have been called upon to be an actor, a friend, a nurse and a doctor, a coach, a finder of lost objects and a money lender, a taxi driver, a therapist and a substitute parent, a salesman, a politician and a keeper of the faith.

Despite all the maps, charts and formulae, verbs, stories and books we have really had nothing to teach because our students have only one thing to learn: who they are, and we know it takes a whole lifetime to find that out.

We are a paradox. We speak loudest when we listen most. Our greatest giving is in what we are willing to receive appreciatively from our students. Our greatest teaching arises out of what we are willing to learn.

Material wealth is not our main goal, rather we are full-time treasure seekers in a quest for new opportunities for our students to use their talents, and help us to expand ours.

We are the most fortunate of all who labour:

A doctor is allowed to usher life into the world in one magic moment.

We are allowed to see that life and new ways of living are reborn each day, with new questions, new ideas and new relationships.

An architect knows that if she builds with care then her structures may stand for centuries. As teachers we know that if we build with Love and Truth, then what we build can last forever.

We can choose to see ourselves as warriors doing battle against peer pressure, negativity, fear, conformity, prejudice, ignorance apathy (and some might say OFSTED). But if we are warriors we have great allies also: intelligence, curiosity, creativity, individuality, love and laughter all rush to our banner with indomitable support.

And who do we have to thank for this vocation, this living, this life we are fortunate to experience. We can thank ourselves for the passion we've put into our work, we can thank the pupils for their persistence, and finally we can thank the public, the parents who trust us enough to send their children to us.

We have a past, which is rich in bitter/sweet, despairing and inspiring memories.

We have a present, which is challenging, adventurous and fun.

We have such a past and such a present because we are allowed to spend our days with those who are the future.

We are teachers

We are learners too

We can appreciate our good fortune every day we stand in front of a class

And We Thank God For It.

Written by John Wayne Schlatter in *Chicken Soup For The Soul Vol. 1*
Adapted and anglicised from John Wayne Schlatter, by Ian Berry[4]

ENTHUSIASM

JOY

WISDOM

VISION

HIGHER GOAL

Chapter 13

Activities to develop Emotional Intelligence

The way to develop empathy is to improve emotional literacy – the ability to recognise the level of feeling, be able to name it and get to know it.

When children learn to recognise and express their emotions in a group, they begin to understand their own emotions, the emotions of others and what affects these emotions. They start to realise that we all have the same emotions, yet we are all affected by them in different ways.

1 Rating feelings

Objective
Children to begin sharing about their feelings in a safe way.

Activity
Introduce children to the rating scale by asking them to rate how they feel on a scale of one to ten.

Extension
This activity can be done each morning and afternoon when you call the register.

2 Naming feelings

Objective

Children to begin naming their feelings and sharing these in a group.

Activity

Initially, children need to be able to say how they feel. Sitting in a circle passing around the 'talking stick', children complete the sentence 'I feel ....'

Extension

This can also be used as a way of answering the register.

3 Naming shades of feeling

Objective

Children to become aware of multiple feelings and to develop emotional literacy.

Activity

1   Make a continuum with pieces of card that have feelings written on them; for example, angry, upset, sad, calm, bored, happy, excited.

2   Ask the children to stand on the one that is closest to their feelings right now.

3   When they are in the line, ask them if anyone has a feeling that is not on the cards that they would like to share.

4   Brainstorm feeling words and display them.

Extension

During the weeks that follow, allow children to add to the list using a dictionary and thesaurus.

4 Alien visit

Objectives

Children to

☘ develop an awareness of the sort of language used around them every day in school.

☘ begin to reflect on how they feel about it.

☘ begin to see that they have a choice about their contribution to the environment by the language they choose to speak.

Activity

1   Tell the children this story:

'One day a space ship comes to visit the school. It hovers closer and closer and then beams some of the aliens into the school. They can cloak themselves in an invisible cloak and walk about the school without anyone seeing them. They have come on a mission to find out how Earth children talk to each other. As they walk around the classrooms, what sort of positive, friendly things would they hear children saying to each other?'

2   In groups, children can discuss the sorts of positive language that the aliens would hear; for example, 'I like you', 'That's a beautiful drawing', 'Thank you for letting me play with you', 'You are a very good friend'.

3   Then discuss in groups what sort of negative language the aliens would hear; for example, 'You're not my friend', 'I'm going to hit you', 'I don't like you', 'You're stupid'.

Questions to ask:

❀   What sort of words do we use?

❀   What sort of effects do they have?

Extension

Children note in their journals during the week the sorts of positive language they have said to other people.

5 What affects our feelings?

Objectives

Children to begin to recognise the effect their behaviour has on others' feelings and the effect others' behaviour can have on their feelings.

Activity: IALAC

1   Read the story IALAC and ask all the children to listen.

IALAC story (I Am Lovable And Capable)

Tamara gets up one morning. It's a lovely sunny morning and she feels great. She takes extra care getting ready and does her hair in a slightly different style. She goes downstairs.

Mother: You're late! What have you done to your hair?

Tamara has her breakfast, collects her things and heads for the door. As she's going out she calls back:

>   Is it OK if I go to Jane's after school? It'll only be for an hour. She wants me to hear a new CD she's just got.

Father: That's right! Spend as much time as you can away from home. After all we've done for you ... all you ever think of is yourself.

At school Tamara is talking excitedly to her friends about a piece of work she is doing. The teacher looks up.

Teacher: What is all that noise? Have you girls no self-control? Didn't I tell you to work quietly? You just don't listen!

Later in school a teacher is handing back some work. She comes to Tamara's.

Teacher: This is much better than last time; a real improvement. You can't have done it by yourself. Who helped you with it?

Walking home from school Tamara is with Jane and a few friends.

Jane: Well, who's coming back to listen to the CD then? Tamara?

Tamara: I can't. My Dad wants me to get back and spend time with them.

Jane: Daddy's little girl eh! Can't go out on her own. Come on then the rest of you. We'll go and have some fun.

2 When they have listened, relate this to the discussion in Activity 2: Naming feelings. Put two circles or boxes in the centre of a circle. Ask the children to put a sparkly star in one box whenever they think the person in the story feels good and a stone in the other box when they think the person in the story feels bad. *Re-read the story.*

a) Why did they put the stars in the box when they did? What do they think the person was feeling?

b) Why did they put the stone in the box when they did? What do they think the person was feeling?

3 Discuss the consequences of what we say to each other.

Activity: Round

Children sit in a circle and take turns to finish the following sentence: 'One thing that causes me to feel angry or upset or sad and so on in school is...' To help children concentrate and listen to each other's contribution, it is useful to pass a special (talking stick) object around. The child with the object talks and everyone else listens.

Extension

1 In a group or individually, children write a short story similar to IALAC that shows the character being affected both positively and negatively.

2 a) Children make the letters IALAC and every time something hurtful or negative is said during the story they tear off a letter.

b) Each time something good happens they put a letter back.

c) Then the children can have a badge they wear for a day. Every time an unkind or hurtful thing is said or done to them they tear off a letter, every time a positive thing is done or said they put one back or decorate the badge a little. The challenge is that the whole class ensure that everyone keeps their badges intact. As a class, you check the progress a few times per day.

6 How are feelings expressed?
Changing your inner state

Objectives

❀ To begin to recognise how we express our feelings in everyday actions.

❀ To begin to recognise feelings in others.

❀ To begin to see the connection between thoughts and feelings and that we can manage them and change our state.

Activity

1   Share any new 'feelings' word that the children may have brought in. Explain that there are eight basic feelings: fear, anger, joy, sadness, acceptance, disgust, expectation and surprise. And that there are hundreds of shades of these! So, for example:

Angry = frustrated, boiling, raging, annoyed, irritated

Joy = happy, delighted, excited, pleased, glad.

2   Introduce children to a game that will allow them to experience different feelings and to change them at will.

a)   Ask the children to walk around in the circle, being careful not to bump into each other.

b)   Call out a feeling and everyone has to walk as if they have that feeling. Do this long enough for some children to begin to really experience the feeling. If there are too many children to do this, make the circle bigger.

c)   Change the feeling. Do three or four feelings and watch. Which ones did they find easy to feel? Which ones did they find difficult?

Questions to ask:

❀ What did we do that game for? To become more aware of feelings.

❀ Are feelings hard or easy to talk about? What makes them hard to talk about?

❀ How do you know when you are feeling a feeling?

❀ Can you stop or change your feelings?

❀ What did that game teach you?

Extension

For the next week start each morning or afternoon with this exercise. Ask the children to sit comfortably and close their eyes, then ask them to concentrate on their body. Take them through the various parts from the feet up to the head and ask them:

❀ 'Is there any area that draws your attention, or part that feels tense, or just attracts you?'

❀ 'Take your concentration to that part of your body. What does it feel like? If you were to give the feeling a name, what name would you give it?'

❀ 'What colour, shape, size is the feeling, what temperature? Is it rough, smooth, heavy or light?'

❀ 'Now imagine you take this feeling outside your body for a moment. See it outside you. Notice the colour, size, shape, temperature. Do you want to change it in any way? Do you want to change the colour? The size? The shape? The temperature? OK then – change it to how you would like it to be.'

❀ 'When you have changed it to exactly what you want, put it back inside. See how it feels now. What name would you call it now?'

❀ 'Now open your eyes.'

7 Reading body language

Objectives

❀ To further develop children's ability to read body language and recognise the emotional state of others.

❀ To develop a safe group and a fun working environment.

Activity: Charades

Play charades acting out emotion words.

Children take it in turns to stand in the middle of a circle of children and act out an emotion; the rest of the class have to guess the emotion.

You can use the words you have gathered in earlier activities as a prompt.

Activity: Brainstorm

Remembering the rule of brainstorm, this activity can be done with the teacher or adult scribing, or as a group with a child or children scribing.

What are the kinds of non-verbal ways we communicate our feelings – body language, tone, expression, volume of voice, gestures? 85 per cent of our emotional communication is non-verbal.

Ask children to try saying phrases like 'Go away', 'You don't mean it', 'Give me that', 'I'll show you' using a variety of tones to express anger, sarcasm, affection, good humour, astonishment.

Extension

Create a 'feelings' collage or 'feelings' painting/drawing.

8 Evoking emotions

Objective

To develop further children's ability to change emotional state. Children begin to see the connection between the external environment and their state. They also see how much control they have over it.

Activity

1 Play music of different sorts and ask the children how the music felt. Children can bring in music of their own that causes them to feel things. You can also use photos, pictures, sounds and stories.

2 Point out the differences and similarities in what children are feeling.

3 Ask children what they have learned about their feelings from this exercise.

Extension

❀ During the week, ask children to practise changing their state to be ready for particular activities.

❀ Help them to change their thoughts and see what happens. For example, remember the girl in Chapter 4. She said to me, 'that girl over there is looking at me, she puts me off, she hates me' and I replied, 'what if she is looking at you because she likes you and would really like to be your friend? What would you do then?' I told her to think about it and let me know what happened. She smiled at the girl the next time she looked, the girl smiled back and both their inner states changed.

9 Sources of feelings

Objectives

Children to practise becoming aware of patterns of behaviour, seeing what triggers different feelings so they can begin to change them.

Activity

1 Children do a round and finish the sentence: 'I am feeling ... because ...'

2 Discuss the concept that we are all responsible for our own feelings, we have control over them.

3 Now try saying: 'I am making myself feel ...' or 'I am allowing ... behaviour to affect me and I am making myself feel ...'

Extension

Ask children to keep a journal for a week and write in it, 'I am making myself feel ...' or the second sentence.

Chapter 14

Activities to support changes in behaviour patterns and clear communication

Why and how the activities work

> Opiate reactors are by far the densest in the frontal lobes of the cerebral cortex of the human brain, which shares many connections with the amygdala ... As Paul emphatically tapped his forehead in front of his frontal cortex – the most newly evolved of the brain structures, and the one that is most fully developed in human beings – I thought about the physiological and biochemical pathways that had had to be forged between that cortex and the rest of the brain to enable humans to learn to control their emotions and act unselfishly. Although the capacity for learning is to some extent present even in the simplest creatures, willpower is the uniquely human 'ghost in the machine', and Paul was sure that it resided only in the frontal cortex.
>
> Candace Pert[1]

One way to support children and adults to build more and more conscious connections between the amygdala and the frontal cortex is to teach them conflict resolution skills. (This will also have an effect on their ability to think optimistically.)

Using these thought processes will alter the automatic responses that often occur in reaction to conflict. Many adults will say they cannot handle conflict: they freeze, or flee, or get very angry. This lack of control over their reactions sometimes causes people to avoid conflict at the cost of their safety, self-respect or future learning.

How many teachers have a queue of children after every break with stories of upset and fights?

'MISS!!!!! Mary said my mum was stupid.'

'Charlie took my ball.'

'They wouldn't let me play.'

'It's not fair!'

'No one likes me.'

What do we as teachers say in response to these? Are our answers helping children to learn? Or are we, at best, putting 'sticky plaster' over them instead of dealing with the underlying causes?

The skills children develop in conflict resolution are useful to them in many ways: as they learn to talk things through, their level of communication of thoughts and feelings is developed; they learn to take turns, listen, understand, analyse, think critically, brainstorm solutions, predict outcomes, make decisions, develop plans and test them out in real life. This is part of the citizenship curriculum and will enable them to participate responsibly in a democratic and culturally diverse society.

The practice of conflict resolution skills allows children to develop empathy skills and to begin to respect others as being as important as themselves. They listen to the feelings and needs of others and work together to reconcile their difficulties. This will develop their ability to be open, honest and compassionate with others.

If we look at the Big Picture, developing good conflict resolution skills will foster a generation of people who can listen to others and work out conflict in a non-violent and respectful way. This could have a huge effect on relationships in the home and at work, both nationally and internationally.

The key steps for resolving conflict

There are seven key steps for resolving conflict:

1 Stop. Cool off (managing inner state, self-control).

2 Talk and listen to each other (responsibility, communication).

3 Find out how you both feel (empathy, self-awareness).

4 Find out what you both need (reflection, tolerance, active listening).

5 Brainstorm solutions (compromise, forgiveness).

6 Choose an idea that you can both agree on.

7 Make a plan ... stick to it (perseverance, initiative, confidence).

Activities to support development of the above skills and understanding

What do we mean by conflict?

Objectives

- To define the term conflict.
- To recognise that there are different responses to conflict.
- To look at the consequences to each response.
- To understand the seven steps above.

Activity

Children need to understand the terms conflict, disagreement, fight, argument.

1   They can discuss, in pairs, conflicts they have been part of or seen in the playground.

2   Get them to look at the three ways we usually deal with conflict:

   a)   Ignore it (say, 'no I'm fine', when you clearly are not).

   b)   Fight or argue.

   c)   Talk it through, problem solve.

3   Tell a story of a conflict that is common to the playground and have the children discuss, role-play, or write three different endings to the conflict using a, b and c above.

4   Ask them to discuss the feelings that each option causes and the short-term and long-term effects of each option.

5   Discuss the importance of finding peaceful solutions to conflicts.

6   Introduce the seven steps to peaceful conflict resolution.

Causes and effects of conflict

Objectives

- To develop Emotional Intelligence about the common effects of conflict.
- To understand the term 'cooling off', that it is not suppressing emotions but finding ways of releasing them that are not harmful to others.
- To help children identify different strategies for cooling off.
- To establish a cooling-off space in the classroom or school.

Activity: Circle time

Circle time can be used to share feelings that the children experience when things go wrong and there is conflict.

1 Work in pairs where each child takes it in turn to say how they have felt when things go wrong or do not go the way they want them to.

2 Ask the children if they have any ways they use to cool off and calm down.

3 Do a round where each child has a chance to share one way of cooling off that has worked for them.

4 Write these ideas on a large sheet of paper and put them up in the classroom.

Activity: Acknowledging anger

It is important to acknowledge that anger is a very natural feeling to experience when in conflict.

1 Discuss with children safe ways of expressing their anger using running, bouncing a ball or shouting. Sometimes we need to do one of these before we can cool off.

2 Establish a cooling-off area in the classroom and encourage children during the week to try out one of the cooling-off methods. Support must to be given on a daily basis by using reminders, praise and encouragement.

Understanding fight, flight, fear, flock behaviours

Objectives

❀ To understand that anger is often the result of the 'fight, flight, flock, freeze' response to fear.

❀ To understand about behaviour patterns and how they work.

❀ To understand how behaviour patterns can be broken.

Activity

1 Explain to the children how the brain works and about the limbic brain's response to fear (see Chapters 3 and 4).

2 Ask the children to think of the last time they felt themselves being triggered into anger. Ask what was happening and help them to recognise the pattern and at what point they could break the pattern (see Chapters 3 and 4).

3 Explain the six seconds way of staying in the neo-cortex (see page 47).

4 Ask children to practise finding the point before they feel the surge of anger and thinking a different thought.

Extension

Children can get into pairs and support each other during the week to 'Think The Thought' instead of reverting to their usual reaction.

Using 'I' statements

Objective

❀ To use 'I' statements as a way of expressing feelings assertively but not aggressively.

❀ To understand that 'I' statements are another way of staying in the neo-cortex and not getting trapped by the amygdala.

Resources

Make a copy of the text shown on page 160 so that it is large enough for all to see and give one copy to each child in the class.

Activity

1 Work with the children to develop the use of 'I' statements by using role-play. Think of the sort of communications that are sometimes made; for example, 'Stop it!', 'You always spoil things', 'Get out of here'.

2 Ask the children how it feels when those things are said to them.

3 Get children to role-play the same situations but this time using 'I' statements to communicate the feelings.

Extension

During the week everyone is asked to practise using 'I' statements and to offer support to each other to do so.

'I' Message

I_____
(feeling)

when you_____
(specific behaviour)

because_____
(how it affects me)

Example: 'I feel *frustrated* when you *interrupt* because *then I can't finish what I want to say.*'

The importance of timing and presentation when communicating upset feelings

When is a good time to give someone an 'I' message? _____

When would be a bad time? _____

What tone of voice would be the most effective in helping the person hear what you say?

_____

More ways of using 'I' messages:

I don't like it when you_____because_____

I feel_____when you_____

When you_____ I feel_____because_____

It's a problem for me when you_____because_____

It bothers me when you_____because_____

I would like_____

(what would make the situation better for me)

I would appreciate it if you would _____

Please _____

I need_____

Listening to understand

Objectives

- To work on listening skills and develop 'listening to understand'.
- To understand how it feels to be really listened to.
- To understand that listening is an active, not a passive, activity

Activity

1 Ask children to work in pairs. One child will be A and the other B.

2 Child A tells child B about something they are interested in. Child B has to show child A that he is not listening.

3 Ask A to feedback what that felt like. Children often say things like, 'I couldn't keep going' or 'There seemed no point so I stopped'.

4 The children swap over so that they both feel what it is like.

5 Next A tells B something that interests them and B shows A that he is really listening and really interested.

6 Observe the children and note the language and the body language. Ask A how it felt when B listened and how A knew that B was listening.

7 Feedback to them what you observed.

8 Swap over and let A listen.

Extension

In all books on circle time there are lots of activities to practise listening skills.

Finding solutions together

Objectives

- To be able to look at problems as needs, 'usually someone's needs are not being met'.
- To practise brainstorming skills.
- To practise evaluating solutions so that there is a win–win conclusion.
- To agree a way of creating a time for upsets between pupils to be resolved.

Activity

Children practise saying what they need and to listen to what others need. They begin to understand that two people's conflicting needs can sometimes cause problems.

1 Ask the children to work in groups of three and role-play one child wanting to listen to music and another needing quiet, or one child playing football in an area where others want to sit and talk.

2 The third child is the negotiator and has to get each of the pair to listen to the other's needs.

3 They write down all the suggested solutions.

4 Help the pair to agree the solution they think is the most fair.

Children need to practise stating their needs, listening to others, brainstorming solutions and finding the solutions that are fair to both parties.

Case study: talk time story

Recently I observed a Year 2 class just after lunch. The children came in and sat on the carpet in a circle, the teacher took the register and then said, 'Now we'll have five minutes talk time.' I wondered what this was and found it delightful. Children put up their hands and the teacher chose who would speak. The chosen child stood up and said, 'I'd like to thank Mary for letting me play with her.' Then Mary stood up and said, 'You're very welcome!'

The next child stood up and said, 'Thank you, John, for talking to me at lunch time.' Then John stood up and said, 'That's OK.'

This went on and then one boy stood up and said, 'Tom, you pushed me into the wall and I felt really upset.' Tom stood up and said, 'Yes, and you tripped me up and I felt angry.'

The teacher asked them how they felt now and they said, upset and angry. She asked them what they could do now to sort it out, and they shrugged. She asked the others and got four or five suggestions. She then said, 'I'll leave you to think about the suggestions and check before break.'

This whole 'talk time' only took five minutes and the children were already learning how to acknowledge each other and to problem solve.

Compromise

Objectives

❀ To help children see that the problem is about people's needs not being met.

❀ To practise producing lots of alternative ways of acting.

❀ To practise evaluating and choosing solutions that work for all.

❀ To support the children in establishing a routine of talking it out when there are disputes.

❀ To establish rules for talking it out.

Activity

1   Finding out what each person needs.

a)   Explain that when there is conflict it is often because people want/need different things.

b)   Use the following scenario as an example and then children can come up with their own ideas to practise the following part on other occasions.

i)   I am humming because it helps me to concentrate and focus. You are working beside me and the humming is distracting you and stopping you from thinking. My need is to hum and I find it impossible to do this activity and concentrate if I have to remember to be silent. This is a problem and a possible source of conflict.

ii)   To solve the problem I must find out your needs. You want to work in silence and you can't think when there is noise.

iii)   Summarise the problem in terms of need. By looking at both our needs we can fully understand and see the Big Picture/The Whole.

2   Tell the children that now we have found out what both people need it is time to brainstorm solutions.

a)   Ensure they are clear about the rules of brainstorming:

❀   Everyone's contribution is valued and written down.

❀   No discussion takes place during the brainstorm.

❀   There is a free flow of ideas as quickly as possible

b)   Encourage the children to come up with as many ideas as possible, remembering *no ideas are stupid*.

3   Children now need to choose the idea they both like best.

a)   Half the class could be person one and the other half person two. Go through the various suggestions and the class put a smiley face if they think their person would like that idea and a frown face if they would not. They can put a straight face if it is OK but not what they would choose.

b)   Then ask which idea was best for both of them.

4   Children need to make a plan and then do it.

❀   Look at which idea they want to go into the plan first.

❀   Then what?

❀   Who will do what? When? Where?

❀   Make it all very specific.

❀   Then the children agree to do what is on the plan and try it.

5   Pretend the plan didn't work very well.

❀   Explain that you can go back to the brainstorm, choose a different idea and plan again.

❀   Or, go back to 2 and redefine the problem.

Activities to develop intrinsic motivation

1 Circle time: publicly stating one's beliefs and values

Objective

To give all the children a chance to express a belief.

Activity

1 Everyone in the room sits in a circle on chairs.

2 The teacher explains that everyone in turn will finish the sentence in a way that is true for them.

   ❀ Children who are not used to doing circle time need to practise listening to each other and this will take time. Passing something like a talking stick around the circle is very effective.

   ❀ It is important that children understand that the job they perform when they do not have the stick is as important as the one they perform when they do have it.

   ❀ Thanking each child as they speak needs to be followed by thanking the children for listening, so they see each is valued. This is the beginning of building safety and respect.

   ❀ It is also important that each child receives thanks for their response and is not judged or evaluated. 'Thank you, Sam' is all that is needed, not 'good answer' or 'sensible answer'.

3 Begin with sentences that are not sensitive – this is another important aspect of safety. Some examples are:

   ❀ I think the weather today is ...

   ❀ My favourite colour is ...

- ❀ When I woke up today I felt …

- ❀ When I go home I think I'll …

- ❀ The sun is shining and …

- ❀ It's windy so …

4 Next use sentences that deal with valuing, looking for alternatives, evaluating alternatives, choosing freely, being proud of one's beliefs. Some examples are:

- ❀ All on my own I can …

- ❀ I like …

- ❀ I'm good at …

- ❀ I'm proud of …

- ❀ What worries me is …

- ❀ Something I do well is …

- ❀ Something I'm proud of is …

- ❀ If I could change the world, I would …

- ❀ If I could have one wish, I would wish …

- ❀ My favourite TV programme is … because …

- ❀ I think fights are …

- ❀ Something I decided for myself this week was …

- ❀ In five years I will be …

- ❀ Friends ought to …

- ❀ Something I can do now that I couldn't do last month (week, year) is …

- ❀ A choice I made that I am proud of is …

- ❀ I keep healthy by …

- ❀ I keep safe by …

- ❀ The things I value most are …

2 Lifeline: knowing and being proud of who you are

Objective

Children to identify the important milestones in their lives so far, to celebrate their achievements and to recognise themselves as capable.

Activity

1 Children draw a line down the centre of a page, one end represents their birth and the other some time in the future or now.

2 On the left side of the line they write all their achievements up to now, and on the right side they write what those achievements have enabled them to do, or

how they have affected their lives. The lifeline can also go on into the future and the child can look at what she wants to achieve, how that will affect her life and what it will enable her to do or feel.

3   Children usually need some support, so brainstorm the sorts of achievements they have accumulated up to now; for example, learned to talk, walk, feed myself, dress myself, ride a bike, swim, dance, write my name, and so on.

4   Adults can model the exercise by doing their own lifeline, which the children usually enjoy.

3 Corners: publicly showing your choices

Objective

Children to make a choice and publicly show what that choice is.

Resources

Four large cards marked A, B, C and D are placed in the four corners of the room.

Activity

1   Ask the children to listen to a statement that gives a number of choices in a particular situation.

2   After considering the choices, the children move to the corner of the room that denotes their choice.

Statements:

a) What would you rather do at the weekend?

Stand in corner A if the answer is go to the seaside.

Stand in corner B if the answer is play a sport.

Stand in corner C if the answer is sleep.

Stand in corner D if the answer is go shopping.

b) Which season do you like the best?

A if the answer is spring.

B if the answer is summer.

C if the answer is autumn.

D if the answer is winter.

c) If you were the headteacher would you:

A   abolish homework.

B   let every one wear what they want to school.

C   introduce really great school dinners.

D   make the playground really interesting.

d) What is the worse thing that could happen to you?

    A being poor.

    B being very ill.

    C being disabled.

    D having no friends.

e) Who would you tell if you have something worrying you?

    A your mum.

    B your dad.

    C your best friend.

    D your teacher.

f) Would you like to have:

    A one really good friend.

    B lots of friends.

    C two or three good friends.

    D a very best friend.

4 Continuum: showing your opinion on an issue

Objectives

❀ Children to think about their own opinions on issues and to recognise that there are a range of opinions.

❀ Children to be able to look at their opinions and freely change them if they so wish.

Resources

❀ Two large cards marked 'A' and 'B', or 'Agree' and 'Disagree', or 'Yes' and 'No.'

❀ A line on the floor.

Activity

This activity can be used to look at a variety of issues ranging from bullying or name calling to drugs, sex or the law.

1   Read out the statements, telling the children what the ends of the line represent.

2   Use simple statements at first and more complex ones as the children become more confident. Remember children in the early stages of development tend to see things in black or white, right or wrong.

Examples of issues or questions:

- ❀ You should always tell the truth.
- ❀ Friends are always there for each other.
- ❀ It is important to stay in places you know are safe.
- ❀ Some drugs should be legalised.
- ❀ Young people know enough about relationships.
- ❀ There is not enough chance for children to give opinions in school.

3 Children stand on the line at a position where they feel their opinion lies.

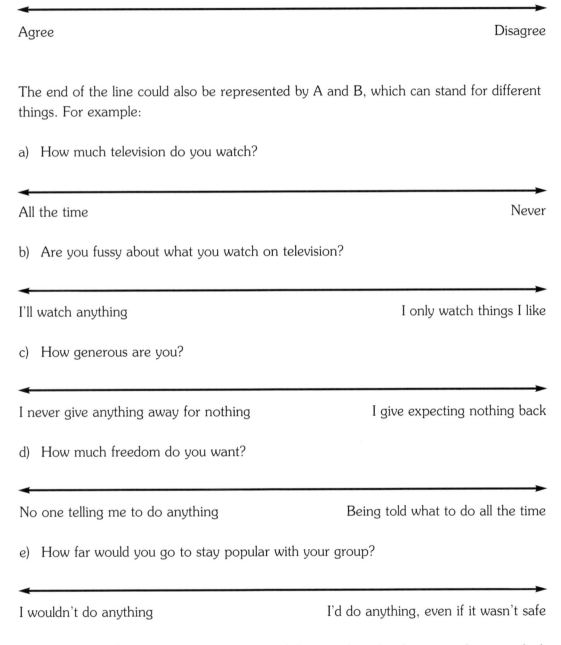

Agree   Disagree

The end of the line could also be represented by A and B, which can stand for different things. For example:

a) How much television do you watch?

All the time   Never

b) Are you fussy about what you watch on television?

I'll watch anything   I only watch things I like

c) How generous are you?

I never give anything away for nothing   I give expecting nothing back

d) How much freedom do you want?

No one telling me to do anything   Being told what to do all the time

e) How far would you go to stay popular with your group?

I wouldn't do anything   I'd do anything, even if it wasn't safe

There are lots of statements you can use and they can be related to topics being studied in any area of the curriculum or current affairs.

5 Brainstorming: creating alternatives

Objective
To generate lots of alternatives quickly.

Resources
- ❀ Flip chart
- ❀ Paper

Activities
If children are not used to brainstorming, then the rules need to be made clear:

1 Every contribution is written down.

2 Every contribution has equal value.

3 Contributions are written in such a way that none are better than others because they have a higher position.

4 No comments are made about the contributions during the brainstorm.

5 The contributions are recorded exactly as they are said.

- ❀ Children need to be reminded of these rules each time they use brainstorming as a process. Do not expect the children to remember the rules as it takes most adults quite a long time to remember them. It is important to wait for the children to think and to give them time to 'buzz' as the auditory learners may need to discuss their ideas before offering them.

- ❀ Brainstorms enable children to think of alternatives quickly; for example, I use them for problem solving, 'What ways do people use to stop themselves hitting someone when they are angry?'

- ❀ They can also be used for looking at why things happen; for example, 'What are the reasons people take drugs?'

- ❀ At the end of the brainstorm the ideas can be discussed and questions asked to clarify understanding.

6 Group work: choosing from alternatives

Objective

To allow children to think about making choices.

Resources

❀ The brainstorm completed in activity 5.

❀ A sheet where they can write down some of the suggestions and what they will do. For example:

Suggestion	Will try it	Will think about it	Don't like it
Think about something funny	Bob	Tess	Gita
Walk away	Mike	David	Sophie

Activity

1 In groups the children consider the alternatives that were put forward in the brainstorm and they choose the one they are willing to try.

2 The heading at the top of the sheet needs to match the topic being brainstormed. For example: Ways of cooling down – choices sheet.

7 Group work: thinking about consequences

Objective

Children are given a chance to consider the consequences of actions.

Resources

❀ Brainstorm from activity 5.

❀ A sheet to record outcomes of discussion. For example:

Suggestion	Positive consequence	Negative consequence
To relieve pain	Pain goes	Might damage more because you can't feel it

Activity

This exercise allows children to learn the skills of evaluation. They can see that there are often positive and negative consequences to many choices. They need lots of practice at weighing up the consequences and choosing what fits their values.

8 Group work: looking at long-term and short-term consequences of our choices

Objective

Children are able to see that sometimes short-term consequences are very different to long-term, and they practise choosing.

Resources

- ❀ Dilemma cards
- ❀ A sheet to record the effects of their choices

Sample recording sheet:

Choice number one	Short-term	Effects on me	Effects on others
Choice number one	Long-term	Effects on me	Effects on others

Activity

1 Children work in small groups of three or four and are given a dilemma to discuss. Examples of possible dilemmas:

- ❀ You know your best friend has started smoking, he has asthma and you are concerned about the effect it will have on your friend's health.

- ❀ You have seen a boy in your class taking something from the cupboard and put it in his bag. Your teacher has mentioned that things are going missing from the stock cupboard and she is very upset.

- ❀ Your parents have heard that your best friend's father has been diagnosed with AIDS and they have told you to stay away from her and not to invite her home any more. She is very upset and worried about her dad.

2 Ask the children to come up with three possible courses of action. For the first example they usually say:

a) Talk to him and say you are worried.

b) Tell his mum or dad.

c) Tell him you will tell on him if he doesn't stop.

d) Mind your own business.

e) Say you won't be his friend any more if he carries on.

The age of the children usually determines the sort of response. The older children are usually more likely to suggest a).

3 The children record the three options they have discussed and the short-term effects on them and others.

4 Children record the long-term effect on themselves and others.

5 They make a choice about which option they would choose given the long-term and short-term effects.

Looking at long-term effects of our actions is something many adults are not very practised at doing. We often behave in ways that relieve the situation now but in the long term will have a very detrimental effect on those around us or ourselves.

Case study: Alex's story

This exercise was used with a Year 6 class. One of the groups was made up of two very quiet and amiable girls and a very loud and angry boy, Alex. He was not pleased that he had ended up in a group with these two girls – it did nothing for his 'street-cred'.

They were given the following dilemma:

You have a girl in your class who is different from the rest of you. Most people in the class ignore her but some tease and torment her. Your teacher approaches you one day and asks you if you will befriend this girl as the teacher is concerned about her.

At first Alex didn't even want to discuss the issue. He said, 'There's nothing to discuss. I wouldn't do it.'

The girls, on the other hand, had already made up their minds to do the opposite. They asked to go through the task even so, and they did. The three options they came up with were:

1 Do what the teacher asked and be friends with her.
2 Ignore the teacher and do what you have always done.
3 Talk to your friends and see if you can get them all to be friends with her.

The following table shows the process Alex went through to make his choice.

Short-term effects ...		
	... on Alex	... on the girl
Option 1	He felt his friends would all think he was mad and would probably start calling him names as well.	She would have a friend, but both of them would now be teased and tormented.

Short-term effects (cont.) …		
	… on Alex	… on the girl
Option 2	Everything would be as it was now. He would be fine.	She would be the same; she would not know he had been asked so nothing would have changed.
Option 3	Would be the same as option one. His friends would think he was mad and turn on him.	She wouldn't know any different.

Long-term effects …		
	… on Alex	… on the girl
Option 1	He would have no friends at all and would be as sad as the girl.	She would not be a lot better off because she would have a friend who was miserable and wanted his other friends back.
Option 2	He would be fine as he was now.	She would be miserable (here is where Alex began to really empathise) and the longer it went on the worse it would be. She would get depressed and maybe even want to kill herself. He then said, 'I know what it feels like to be that miserable. I've thought about killing myself you know.'
Option 3	His friends would think he was mad … but then he thought about it for a moment and said that if he told them how it felt, then they might understand.	She could have lots of friends if he could make them see.

Alex decided in the end that he would choose option 3. When we came back together as a whole class, he shared with the class how he came to that decision. From that day on the whole class treated him with much more respect and he began to show a very different aspect of himself.

The two girls also decided to choose option 3.

9 Values cards or balloons: looking at what is valuable to you

Objective

To enable children to discuss the things that are important to them.

Resources

Values cards or picture of balloon with bags of ballast.

Activity

If using the picture of a balloon, the bags of ballast can have labels on them such as health, family, fresh air, holidays, beauty, food, friends, money, happiness.

The cards can also have the same, or older children can write their own, which should be the five things they most value.

1 If using the balloon, tell the children that the balloon is approaching a mountain that is very high. They need to drop a bag of ballast to enable them to lighten the balloon and rise up. Which bag do they drop?

2 Go on with the exercise for as long as you wish and drop as many bags as you need to. The children have a very hard time deciding what to throw out.

3 At the end, children can discuss in groups what they got rid of and what it felt like.

   a) Which one was the hardest to give up?

   b) Why did you keep the one you kept till last?

Extension

Follow-up activities can include:

1 To look at your life and see if you act as if these are the most important things to you.

2 To look at the kinds of behaviour that might cause you to lose these things.

3 Children can choose one of the things they value the most and design an aspiration poster that shows 'what I will see, hear, feel when I am acting as if this is really important'.

4 Children then produce an action plan for getting there using milestones along the way.

Healthy choices, drug prevention and sex education have been included in this sort of exercise. Young people get a chance to look at the long-term consequences of some of their choices and see that they might finish up losing that which they value the most, for example, freedom. This is not the end and the young people still need support to give up some of the behaviours they have adopted, but now the motivation is intrinsic.

Chapter 16

Activities to develop a sense of identity

These activities are designed to enable children to develop an awareness of themselves, to know who they are and who they want to be. They help children to see the roles they play and the masks they wear. This gives them an insight into the person they are showing to the world and, therefore, a choice over how they are going to present that person.

1 Group identity: beginning to feel safe

Objectives

- ❀ To begin contact within the group.
- ❀ To develop safety.
- ❀ To develop a sense of group identity.

Activity

1 Set the scene: they are at a station and it is quite busy. They do not know anyone so they deliberately avoid looking at anyone.

2 Ask the children to walk around the room as if it were the railway station and not to look at anyone. They are in a rush, so they get through the crowd as quickly as possible and do not bump into anyone.

3 Make sure everyone understands what to do, which is to walk around the room ignoring everyone.

4 Stop. Now ask them to reflect on how it felt to not look at anyone and to keep walking away from people as they walked towards you.

5 Keeping those questions in mind, ask them to begin walking around as before.

6   Stop. Reflect on the experience. After a few moments ask them to walk around the room again but this time making eye contact with everyone they pass. Ask them to notice their thoughts and feelings.

7   Stop and reflect on the experience.

8   This time walk around and as they pass each person do something positive to acknowledge the other's presence. For example, say hello, smile, nod, or shake hands. The children decide which they want to do and try to make contact with as many people as possible.

9   Stop. This time as the children walk around, they stop as they reach each person and tell them their name and something about themselves. Some groups will need support, for example, tell the person your favourite food.

10 Stop. Tell the children to stay with the last person they spoke to and go and sit with them. Ask them to spend a few moments talking about their feelings and thoughts during that exercise.

11 Come back together in a circle and discuss:

   a) How did it feel when you ignored everyone?

   b) What was it like to be ignored?

   c) How was it different when you made eye contact? And then when you acknowledged them and spoke to them?

   d) Which one was easiest for you?

   e) Which one was the most difficult?

   f) What made it easy/difficult?

   g) Was your experience the same as your partner's, or different?

Extension

During the week children should notice where and when they do each of the above, where they are and why they behave as they do. Also notice how it feels.

2 Confidence to speak out in a group

Objectives

   ❀ To help the group introduce themselves.

   ❀ To get to know each other.

   ❀ To encourage co-operation and group interaction.

Activity

1   Ask the children to sit in a circle in alphabetical order. Show them where to begin, in others words, where A will sit.

2   Tell them which direction to go in, that is clockwise.

3   When you are clear they all know what to do and how to do it, tell them to go.

4   Ask them to check with the person either side of them and make sure they are in alphabetical order.

5   Now ask them to mix themselves up again (or play a mix up game).

6   Ask if anyone thinks they can put the class back into alphabetical order.

7   Everyone helps if the volunteer get stuck.

8   Everyone waits until they are told to move by the volunteer.

9   Begin.

10   Back in the circle discuss:

     a)   How difficult did you find that activity?

     b)   How many names were you unsure of? Do you know why?

     c)   What was it like being a volunteer?

     d)   How did it feel when someone got your name wrong or did not remember it?

     e)   How important are names to us? What do you think makes them important?

Extension

There are lots of name games and activities in most circle time books; for example, children find out the reason why their parent(s) picked their name, or they find out the meaning of their name.

3   Getting to know me

Objectives

☘   To allow children to get to know themselves and each other better.

☘   To encourage children to reflect and develop intrapersonal skills.

☘   To encourage thinking in an intuitive way.

Resources

☘   Two pieces of paper or two large index cards for each person

☘   Coloured pens or pencils

☘   Photocopies of ideas sheet (see page 181)

Activity

1   Ask the children to reflect on their favourite colour and what colours they like.

2   Ask them to reflect on what colour best represents how they are feeling right now.

3   If they were to turn into a colour, what colour would it be?

4   Ask them to find a pen or pencil as near to their colour as possible and write their name on the paper in that colour. Ask them to keep it to themselves and not show anyone.

5   Ask the children to walk around and find people who have used the same colour as them and sit together in a group.

6   Do a round where each child completes the following sentence:

I chose the colour ...... because ......

7   Ask children to reflect on the following questions:

a)   Was that easy for you?

b)   What did you think of that activity?

c)   Did your colour reflect your feelings or mood?

d)   What surprised or interested you?

8   Give out the ideas sheet and explain it, then ask the children to use this to help them think of five to eight statements about themselves and write them on the second piece of paper/card (they do not write their name).

9   When the class has finished, ask them to get into groups of four/six/eight, depending on age. The younger the children the smaller the group. Then ask them to place the paper/card in the centre of the group and pick a dealer. The dealer shuffles them and deals them out face down so everyone gets one.

10   Ask them to take it in turns to read out their card and then everyone in the group tries to guess who it is.

11   When they have found out who wrote the card, they return it to the owner.

12   When they all have their cards back, ask them to look at the card again and choose one thing they would like to tell the group about themselves.

13   Then each child has two or three minutes to speak to the group about themselves.

Extension

Ask the class to discuss:

1   What do you remember most about that activity?

2   How did you feel while you were taking part?

3   What surprised you?

4   What did you appreciate about what other people said?

5   What have you learned about others in your group?

6   What have you learned about yourself?

IDEAS SHEET

A time when I was brave was _____

When I was younger I really enjoyed _____

I value _____

I am proud of _____

I am proud that I _____

One of my strengths is _____

I taught someone how to _____

I have learned to _____

I received praise when I _____

A new skill I have learned is _____

I enjoy _____

Something I would like others to know about me is _____

An exciting thing I did was _____

I helped someone else to _____

4 Patterns of privacy and boundaries

Objectives

- ✿ To help children reflect on their patterns of privacy and their boundaries.
- ✿ To look at questions like 'am I too open?' or 'am I too withdrawn/closed?'

Resources

A sheet of concentric circles (see below).

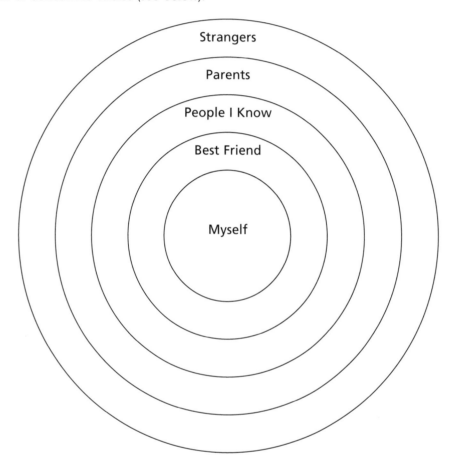

Activity

1. Explain to the children that there are things in our lives we would be glad to tell anyone, we would tell only our friends, we would tell only our parents or we might tell only ourselves.

2. Ask the children to write down the answers to the questions below on the concentric circles sheets.

3. They only write one-word answers. For example, in answer to the question 'Which is your favourite TV programme?', the child would write TV in the circle or circles that show whom they would be willing to tell this information to.

4. You can make up various questions such as:

   a) What you cried about last time you cried (write 'cried' in the appropriate circle).

   b) What you like about your parents (write 'parents +').

Becoming Emotionally Intelligent – Catherine Corrie

c) What you find difficult about your parents (write 'parents –').

d) What you find difficult about your best friend (write 'friend –').

e) If you could change one part of your body, what part would it be (write 'body –').

f) What you think is a spiritual experience (write 'spiritual').

5   The children can work with partners and share as much as they wish about the experience.

5 Who am I really?

Objectives

❀ To allow children to ask the question 'who am I?'

❀ To develop trust in working with a partner.

❀ To reflect on who they are.

Resources

❀ Paper

❀ Pencils

❀ Drawing materials

Activity

1   Allow the children to work with someone with whom they feel comfortable.

2   Ask them to join up with two other couples so there are six.

3   Working with their partner, tell them to look at their partner and ask themselves, 'who is...?'

4   Ask them to think about that question and write down four answers.

5   Ask the pairs to show each other the answers and discuss.

6   In the group of six, ask them to share what it was like and how their partner felt about what they wrote.

7   Ask them to go back to their pairs and pick an A and B. A asks B 'who are you?' and B replies. A writes down the things B said and keeps asking the same question.

8   If B is having difficulty, then A just keeps asking but gives B time to think.

9   A and B swap and do it the other way around.

10 Tell the children to give each other the list they have written down for them and each person reflects on what they said about themselves.

11 Ask them to pick one of the statements that they think reflects how they see themselves right now, and using the drawing materials reproduce the statement in any way they choose.

Extension

Children can share their drawing with a partner if they choose, write something about the experience or they may wish to spend more time on the representation and create a picture, badge or poster. They need to be able to choose what they want do with the experience.

6 Using metaphors: I'd rather be a hammer than a nail

Objective

❀ To use metaphors to encourage children's imagination and allow them to experiment with different images of how they see themselves.

❀ To allow children to see how changing the metaphors we use about ourselves can also change our perceptions of the world.

Resources

Writing material

Activity

1 Introduce the activity by using the children's imagination; for example, 'Imagine you woke up one morning and during the night you had changed into something else.'

2 Tell them it is bad but not as bad as it might be as they have a little choice.

3 You are now going to ask them to choose.

4 Would you rather be:

❀ Hammer or nail

❀ Pleased or sorry

❀ Yes or no

❀ Cat or mouse

❀ Horse or cart

❀ Red or green

❀ Ice cream or jelly

❀ Bacon or eggs

❀ Tree or flower

❀ Rose or buttercup

❀ Swings or roundabout

❀ Chips or chocolate

❀ Forest or stream

❀ Brick or feather

❀ Sparrow or snail.

5   Ask them to compare their answers with others. They will need to be able to walk around and discuss. Ask them to see if they can find anyone who has the same choices as them.

6   When they have found someone, or several people, ask them to sit down and discuss their answers. Why did they choose the ones they did? In what ways are they alike?

7   If anyone cannot find someone the same, they can find either the closest or the opposite.

Extension

Circle discussion on the following questions:

1   What was it like when you compared your answers?

2   Did anything surprise you?

3   What does it feel like to have different answers to everyone else?

4   What did you discover about yourself and others?

7 Me on the inside

Objectives

❀   To develop awareness of the inside and the outside person.

❀   To enable the children to see how much they hide and how safe they feel to show themselves.

Resources

❀   Large sheet of paper, A3 or larger

❀   Art materials

Activity

1   Ask the children to fold the paper down the middle along the width.

2   On one half they are going to represent themselves on the outside and on the other half themselves on the inside.

3   Ask them to think about the colours and shapes they feel would represent the outside person and the inside one. Explain it does not need to look like a person, it can be symbols, signs, shapes that represent them on the inside or the outside.

4   When they have completed the artwork, allow them to discuss it with a friend if they wish.

5   Ask them if there is much of a difference. Do they like it the way it is or would they like to change any of it?

6   See if anyone would like to share and discuss possibilities.

Extension

Some of the children may like to create an aspiration drawing of themselves on the outside/inside or both. Ask them to show how they would feel, what they would sound like and how they would look.

Then help them to decide on steps to get there, small achievable steps by certain dates.

References

Chapter 1

1 Zohar, Danah and Marshall, Ian (2001) *SQ Spiritual Intelligence: The Ultimate Intelligence*, London: Bloomsbury

2 Gottman, John and Declaire, Joan (1998) *Raising an Emotionally Intelligent Child*, Fireside Books

3 Salovey, Mayer, Goldman, Turvey and Palfai (1995) 'Emotional attention, clarity and repair: exploring emotional intelligence using the Trait Meta-mood scale', in *Emotion, Disclosure, and Health*, (ed.) I.J. Pennebaker, Washington DC: American Psychological Association, www.6seconds.org

4 Doyle (1986) www.6seconds.org

5 Rosenfield (1991) www.6seconds.org

6 Stone-McCown, Karen, Jensen, Anabel L., Freedman, Joshua M. and Rideout, Marsha C. (1998) *Self-Science: The Emotional Intelligence Curriculum*, Santa Monica, CA: 6 Seconds

7 Elias, Dr Maurice (1999) 'Emotionally Intelligent Parenting', *EQ Today*, winter, www.6seconds.org

8 Jenson, Eric (1996) *Completing The Puzzle*, Del Mar, CA: The Brain Store Inc, www.6seconds.org

Chapter 2

1 Crocker, William J., Source unknown

2 Zukav, Gary (2001) *The Dancing Wu Li Masters: An Overview of the New Physics*, London: Rider

3 Smith, Alistair and Call, Nicola (2001) *The Alps Approach resource book*, Stafford: Network Educational Press

Chapter 4

1   Pert, Candace (1999) *Molecules of Emotion*, London: Pocket Books

2   Zohar, Danah and Marshall, Ian (2001) *SQ Spiritual Intelligence: The Ultimate Intelligence*, London: Bloomsbury

Chapter 5

1   Chopra, Deepak (1997) *The Path to Love*, New York: Harmony Books

2   Walsch, Neale Donald (1999) *Conversations with God. Book 3*, London: Hodder Stoughton

3   Goleman, Daniel (1996) *Emotional Intelligence: Why It Can Matter More Than IQ*, London: Bloomsbury

4   Mayor, Federico (1995) *A Year for Tolerance*

Chapter 6

1   Leney, Norah, 'Grief', *Good Grief*, London: Jessica Kingsley

2   Stevens, Sophie, 'Anger', *Good Grief*, London: Jessica Kingsley

3   Translation of a poem by a Turkish Girl, *Good Grief*, London: Jessica Kingsley

Chapter 7

1   Burns, Sally and Lamont, Georgeanne (1995) *Values and Visions: A Handbook for Spiritual Development and Global Awareness*, London: Hodder & Stoughton

Chapter 8

1   Assagioli, Roberto (1999) *The Act of Will*, Woking: David Platts Publishing

2   Hartley, Robert (1986) 'Imagine you're clever', *Journal of Child Psychology and Psychiatry*

3   Kumaris, Brahma, *Living Values: A Guidebook*, World Spirituality University

4   Burns, Sally and Lamont, Georgeanne (1995) *Values and Visions: A Handbook for Spiritual Development and Global Awareness*, London: Hodder & Stoughton

Chapter 9

1 Fromm, Erich (2000) *The Art of Loving*, London: Perennial Classics (HarperCollins)

2 NLP NORTHEAST 'Magic Spelling'. Booklet available price £1.00 from NLP NORTHEAST, Bongate Mill Farmhouse, Appleby in Westmorland, Cumbria CA16 6UR

3 Jensen, Eric (1996) *Completing the Puzzle: A Brain-Based Approach to Learning*, Del Mar, CA: The Brain Store Inc.

4 Smith, Alistair and Call, Nicola (2000) *The Alps Approach*, Stafford: Network Educational Press

5 Smith, Alistair (1999) *Accelerated Learning in Practice*, Stafford: Network Educational Press

Chapter 10

1 Carroll, Lewis (1994) *Alice's Adventures in Wonderland*, London: Penguin

2 Millman, Dan (1993) *The Life You Were Born To Live*, Tiburon, CA: Kramer

Chapter 12

1 Burns, Sally and Lamont, Georgeanne (1995) *Values and Visions: A Handbook for Spiritual Development and Global Awareness*, London: Hodder & Stoughton

2 Zohar, Danah and Marshall, Ian (2001) *SQ Spiritual Intelligence: The Ultimate Intelligence,* London: Bloomsbury

3 Guare, John (1990) *Six Degrees of Separation*, London: Random House

4 Berry, Ian 'We are teachers'. Adapted and anglicised from a poem by John Wayne Schlatter (1993) in Jack Canfield and Mark Victor Hansen (eds) *Chicken Soup for the Soul*, Vermilion.

Chapter 14

1 Pert, Candace (1999) *Molecules of Emotion*, London: Pocket Books

Acknowledgements

The publishers wish to thank people and organisations for permission to use extracts from their material in this book. Every effort has been made to contact copyright holders of materials reproduced in this book. The publishers apologise for any omissions and will be pleased to rectify them at the earliest opportunity.

6 seconds and *EQ Today*
Material reproduced with permission from 6 seconds.org and *EQ Today*

Gary Zukav, *The Dancing Wu Li Masters: An Overview of the New Physics*, Rider
Extract used by permission of The Random House Group Limited

Candace Pert, *Molecules of Emotion*, Pocket Books
Extract used by permission of Simon & Schuster

Chopra, Deepak, *The Path to Love*, Harmony Books
Extracts used by permission of Harmony Books, a division of Random House, Inc

Sally Burns and Georgeanne Lamont, *Values and Visions*, Hodder Stoughton
Extracts used by permission of the Manchester Development Education Project

Dan Millman, *The Life You Were Born To Live*, H J Kramer/New World Library
Extract used by permission of H J Kramer/New World Library

Berry, Ian, *We are Teachers*, adapted and anglicised from a poem by John Wayne Schlatter in *Chicken Soup for the Soul,* Vermilion
Extract used by permission of Ian Berry and by permission of John Wayne Schlatter

Index

THE SCHOOL EFFECTIVENESS SERIES

Book 1: *Accelerated Learning in the Classroom* by Alistair Smith
ISBN: 1-85539-034-5

Book 2: *Effective Learning Activities* by Chris Dickinson
ISBN: 1855390353

Book 3: *Effective Heads of Department* by Phil Jones & Nick Sparks
ISBN: 1-85539-036-1

Book 4: *Lessons are for Learning* by Mike Hughes
ISBN: 185539-038-8

Book 5: *Effective Learning in Science* by Paul Denley and Keith Bishop
ISBN: 1-85539-039-6

Book 6: *Raising Boys' Achievement* by Jon Pickering
ISBN: 1-85539-040-X

Book 7: *Effective Provision for Able & Talented Children* by Barry Teare
ISBN: 1-85539-041-8

Book 8: *Effective Careers Education & Guidance* by Andrew Edwards and Anthony Barnes
ISBN: 1-85539-045-0

Book 9: *Best behaviour and Best behaviour FIRST AID* by Peter Relf, Rod Hirst, Jan Richardson and Georgina Youdell
ISBN: 1-85539-046-9

Best behaviour FIRST AID
ISBN: 1-85539-047-7   (pack of 5 booklets)

Book 10: *The Effective School Governor* by David Marriott
ISBN 1-85539-042-6   (including free audio tape)

Book 11: *Improving Personal Effectiveness for Managers in Schools* by James Johnson
ISBN 1-85539-049-3

Book 12: *Making Pupil Data Powerful* by Maggie Pringle and Tony Cobb
ISBN 1-85539-052-3

Book 13: *Closing the Learning Gap* by Mike Hughes
ISBN 1-85539-051-5

Book 14: *Getting Started* by Henry Leibling
ISBN 1-85539-054-X

Book 15: *Leading the Learning School* by Colin Weatherley
ISBN 1-85539-070-1

Book 16: *Adventures in Learning* by Mike Tilling
ISBN 1-85539-073-6

Book 17: *Strategies for Closing the Learning Gap* by Mike Hughes & Andy Vass
ISBN 1-85539-075-2

Book 18: *Classroom Management* by Phillip Waterhouse and Chris Dickinson
ISBN 1-85539-079-5

Book 19: *Effective Teachers* by Tony Swainston
ISBN 1-85539-125-2

Book 20: *Transforming Teaching and Learning*
by Colin Weatherley, Bruce Bonney, John Kerr and Jo Morrison
ISBN 1-85539-080-9

ACCELERATED LEARNING SERIES

General Editor: **Alistair Smith**

Accelerated Learning in Practice by Alistair Smith
ISBN 1-85539-048-5

The ALPS Approach: Accelerated Learning in Primary Schools
by Alistair Smith and Nicola Call
ISBN 1-85539-056-6

MapWise by Oliver Caviglioli and Ian Harris
ISBN 1-85539-059-0

The ALPS Approach Resource Book by Alistair Smith and Nicola Call
ISBN 1-85539-078-7

Creating an Accelerated Learning School by Mark Lovatt & Derek Wise
ISBN 1-85539-074-4

ALPS StoryMaker by Stephen Bowkett
ISBN 1-85539-076-0

Thinking for Learning by Mel Rockett & Simon Percival
ISBN 1-85539-096-5

Reaching out to all learners by Cheshire LEA
ISBN 1-85539-143-0

EDUCATION PERSONNEL MANAGEMENT SERIES

Education Personnel Management handbooks will help headteachers, senior managers and governors to manage a broad range of personnel issues.

The Well Teacher – management strategies for beating stress, promoting staff health and reducing absence by Maureen Cooper
ISBN 1-85539-058-2

Becoming Emotionally Intelligent – Catherine Corrie

Managing Challenging People – dealing with staff conduct by Bev Curtis and Maureen Cooper
ISBN 1-85539-057-4

Managing Poor Performance – handling staff capability issues by Bev Curtis and Maureen Cooper
ISBN 1-85539-062-0

Managing Allegations Against Staff – personnel and child protection issues in schools
by Maureen Cooper
ISBN 1-85539-072-8

VISIONS OF EDUCATION SERIES

The Unfinished Revolution by John Abbott and Terry Ryan
ISBN 1-85539-064-7

The Learning Revolution by Jeannette Vos & Gordon Dryden
ISBN 1-85539-085-X

Wise Up by Guy Claxton
ISBN 1-85539-099-X

ABLE & TALENTED CHILDREN COLLECTION

Effective Resources for Able and Talented Children by Barry Teare
ISBN 1-85539-050-7

More Effective Resources for Able and Talented Children by Barry Teare
ISBN 1-85539-063-9

Challenging Resources for Able and Talented Children by Barry Teare
ISBN 1-85539-122-8

MODEL LEARNING

Thinking Skills & Eye Q by Oliver Caviglioli, Ian Harris & Bill Tindall
ISBN 1-85539-091-4

Class Maps by Oliver Caviglioli & Ian Harris
ISBN 1-85539-139-2

OTHER TITLES FROM NEP

The Brain's Behind It by Alistair Smith
ISBN 1-85539-083-3

Help Your Child To Succeed by Bill Lucas & Alistair Smith
ISBN 1-85539-111-2

Tweak to Transform by Mike Hughes
ISBN 1-85539-140-6

Brain Friendly Revision by UFA National Team
ISBN 1-85539-127-9

Numeracy Activities Key Stage 2 by Afzal Ahmed & Honor Williams
ISBN 1-85539-102-3

Numeracy Activities Key Stage 3 by Afzal Ahmed, Honor Williams & George Wickham
ISBN 1-85539-103-1

Imagine That... by Stephen Bowkett
ISBN 1-85539-043-4

Self-Intelligence by Stephen Bowkett
ISBN 1-85539-055-8

Class Talk by Rosemary Sage
ISBN 1-85539-061-2

Becoming Emotionally Intelligent – Catherine Corrie